Turning Tides

A history of the Tyne and the Wear

Michael W. Marshall

Keepdate Publishing

Keepdate Publishing

Published by Keepdate Publishing Ltd
21 Portland Terrace · Jesmond
Newcastle upon Tyne NE2 1QQ
UK

First Edition 1997

ISBN 1-899506-35-7

Designed and typeset by Keepdate Publishing Ltd, Newcastle upon Tyne.
Printed in Hong Kong.

For Julie and Sylvie

Acknowledgements

Special thanks are due to Rosemary Baker, C. Dubois, J. Hinves, Susan Mills and Colin Rendall for their critical comments during the preparation of the book.

Picture and illustration acknowledgements:

Air photo: page 136

Bede's World, Jarrow: pages 31, 32, 33, 34 bottom, 35, 38

Biblioteca Medicea-Laurenziana, Florence, Italy: page 36

Bibliotheque Nationale, Paris: pages 67, 68, 69, 83

Chris Kent: pages 12, 17, 29, 40, 81, 86

David Bell: pages 34 top, 51

David Temple: page 121, 146

Frank Harris: page 58

Jennifer Hinves: page 46

Laurie Sparham: pages 2, 125 bottom

Michael W. Marshall: pages 2, 3, 4, 5, 10, 13, 15, 16, 22, 24, 25, 26, 28, 44, 45, 56, 57, 61, 62, 66, 139, 148

M E Saltykov-Shchedrin Public Library, St Petersburg. MS Q.V.I .18, f 26v: page 37

Museum of Antiquities of the University and Society of Antiquaries of Newcastle upon Tyne: pages 7, 8, 9, 11 top, 14, 18, 19, 23, 39

National Maritime Museum, London: pages 91, 101

Science Museum: page 20

Tyne and Wear Museums: pages 11 bottom, 97, 99, 111, 122, 126, 127, 129

University of Newcastle upon Tyne, Library: pages 48, 85, 90

Vickers Defence Systems: pages 140, 141, 142

CONTENTS

INTRODUCTION

This book endeavours to take a 'why and therefore' approach to regional history rather than the more conventional factual and chronological method. It also attempts to place the history of the Tyne and the Wear in a wider context: the beginning of each chapter has a national, often international, historical overview before considering the 'Two Rivers'.

It is a complex history and the tide has turned many times for the cities, towns and people of Tyneside and Wearside. Regions and fortune do not evolve in isolation and to understand why in one epoch the North East is riding high to be followed by another when it is hitting the depths of economic and social depression it is necessary to consider many factors. Terrain and natural resources will always affect the development of a region. Mainland British geography, its highlands to the north and west and lowlands to the south and east, had much influence on the economic, social and environmental evolution of the North East as did, since the 1300s, the Tyne and Wear coalfields.

For thousands of years until England, at least, became a united country under William the Conqueror, Britain was unable to present any semblance of a single front against potential invaders. Its open-beached, south and east coast lowlands were an easy prey to any warlike tribe that was prepared to put to sea from any of the coastal states that ringed the North Sea, from Norway through to Normandy. The more impenetrable and more easily defended mountains and hills in the north and west of Britain acted both as refuge and reservoir for 'British' tribes whose lifestyles and cultures were for centuries displaced and or diluted by wave after wave of continental invaders: Celts, Romans, Anglo-Saxons, Vikings and Normans.

Once the country was united, Britain's merchant adventurers sailed and traded round the globe to help create the British Empire, the largest the world has ever seen. Partly due to its natural resources Britain was the first country to industrialise and the first to develop industrial capitalism. It benefited greatly but there were problems, some of which have yet to be solved.

The Tyne and the Wear played, and continue to play, important and leading roles in the rise and gentle decline of the British nation. It is a long story.

North Tyne Head.

The Tyne

The River Tyne has two main tributaries, the North and South Tyne. The North Tyne rises in the Cheviots while the South Tyne rises on Cross Fell in the Pennine Hills. Tyneside's Industrial Revolution depopulated much of this part of the North Tyne valley and today the valley below North Tyne Head is empty and quiet. Everywhere the soil is wet and peaty and there are few remains of the North British Railway Company's line that was built in 1855 when 'railway fever' gripped Victorian Britain. To prevent the single track line from sinking it was laid on tight bundles of local sheep's wool that were forced into the marshy ground before the bundles were covered with hardcore and gravel.

Salmon fisher on the North Tyne above Warden.

Deadwater Burn rises on nearby Peel Fell that towers over the valley and some believe that the Burn is the source of the Tyne. A local sheep farmer disagrees, arguing that for generations his family have considered a small, water-filled hollow down in the valley to be the source where he says, 'there is always water even on the hottest summer day'. The hollow is found in a field, north of the road and about half a mile from the Deadwater Burn which he considers to be the Tyne's first major tributary.

From the fells and the moors of Upper Tynedale the North Tyne flows southwards through the huge reservoir of Kielder Water, that was completed in 1979, to rise high in the air as twin jets of foaming white water form the face of the 170ft high Kielder Dam. Falstone village is about a mile away from the Dam and upstream of the small town of Bellingham. Some 3km downstream of Bellingham the North Tyne is joined by the River Rede and it continues south to meet the South Tyne at Warden.

The source of the South Tyne is close to the source of

the River Wear – about 5km away. The South Tyne has humble beginnings – a small patch of marshy peat, an insignificant part of the high, wide and lonely Cross Fell. The river has few tributaries, fed rather by countless rivulets that run off Tyne Head Fell, Round Hill and Bellbeaver Rigg. The South Tyne gathers force as it flows north, down through the pretty village of Garrigill and then on to Alston beside a track that was once a 'carrier way' for countless pack horses and carts going to and from the local lead mines. For the South Tyne valley, and the valleys of the East and West Allens, make up the 'lead dales' which, with the surrounding high fells and moorlands, were once part of the North Pennine orefield. Lead mines have been worked in the orefield since the times of the Romans.

The North Pennine orefield was once so rich that in the seventeenth and eighteenth centuries it made Britain the world's largest producer of lead and, during the eighteenth and nineteenth centuries, most of the population of the lead dales depended on lead mining. Lead production peaked in the mid-nineteenth century while mining for zinc and other lucrative metals from the orefield reached its height around 1900. There were once over 30 lead mines and mills in the lead dales and, to help bring the ore down to the crushing mills and smelters, the Victorians, with magnificent feats of engineering, built railways: branch lines from the main Newcastle-Carlisle line into the valleys of the Allen and upper South Tyne. The Alston branch line was built in 1856 and crossed the South Tyne at Lambley on a majestic viaduct that still towers over 30m above the river. Lead by the thousands of tons came down in the goods trains – from Allendale to Hexham and from Alston to Haltwhistle – but now the mines of

The source of the South Tyne.

the North Pennine orefield are all worked out. The last major Tyne Basin metal mine closed in 1950.

The South Tyne, after flowing through Alston, turns east through Haltwhistle where it is joined by its major tributary, the River Allen, before passing through Haydon Bridge to meet the North Tyne at Warden, at 'Tyne Waters Meet', to form the main Tyne. The main Tyne flows east through the market town of Hexham and then Corbridge. Corbridge owes its origins to the Romans who built a bridge near the present town and a fort to guard the bridge which carried Dere Street, the main supply route from York, up to the major Roman base of Newstead in Scotland. For most of its way the North, South and main Tynes have flowed over carboniferous limestone, but not far from Corbridge the river encounters millstone grit before quickly running into the coal measures for which Newcastle was once so famous. The grit and the coal are responsible for two world-famous proverbs – both dealing with exports

Cross Fell Moors. Killhope Burn on its way to meet Wellhope Burn: at their confluence the River Wear begins.

The Wear

Killhope Burn and the Wellhope Burn flow down from Cross Fell on the east slopes of the Pennine Hills. They meet and, at their confluence, the River Wear begins. The Burns carry the brown water from the wet, peaty earth of Killhope and Wellhope Moors and, as the Wear flows eastwards, its flow is constantly swelled by more Pennine tributaries, the River Gaunless and the Bedburn Beck, as well as a number of smaller burns and runoffs.

Upper Weardale is criss-crossed by miles of ancient, moss-covered dry stone walls which help create a scenic mosaic of upland farms, woodlands and small villages. Many of the gravelly streams and small tributaries above Bishop Auckland are 'redds', spawning grounds for salmon and sea trout that have returned to the river to breed.

The river flows over carboniferous sandstone, limestone, shale and of course coal. Today the Durham coalfield, once the largest in the world, is no more but it is, indirectly, one of the major contributors to the volume of water in the River Wear. Water is continuously seeping into the hundreds of miles of disused mine workings and is constantly being pumped out and into the Wear. Stopping the minewater pumps could cause serious pollution as salts, particularly

North and South Tynes: the meeting of the waters.

from the Tyne. The medieval proverb is less well known: 'A Scot, a rat and a Newcastle grindstone may be found all the world over'.

The river is tidal at Wylam and downstream from there passes through Newcastle, Gateshead, North and South Tyneside which includes North and South Shields, to enter the sea at Tynemouth and complete a journey of some 56km from Tyne Waters Meet.

Above: Killhope Burn, Upper Weardale.

Right: The Wear begins at the confluence of the Killhope and Wellhope Burns.

iron, become concentrated in the mines to overflow into the river. The dissolved salts in the pumped minewaters already make the water in the Wear estuary particularly 'hard'.

The Wear passes through Cowshill, St John's Chapel, Westgate, Eastgate, Frosterley, Stanhope and Wolsingham before turning north at Bishop Auckland. Just after the confluence of its largest lowland tributary, the River Browney, the Wear makes a great meander loop round the City of Durham before broadening and deepening to wind its way through the coastal plain past the ancient town of Chester-le-Street to meet the sea at Sunderland. The Tyne and the Wear are linked at Frosterley by the Kielder transfer tunnel. The Riding Mill Pumping station on the main Tyne can pump water into the Wear at Frosterley and, in times of drought, the increase in flow rate does much to improve the River Wear's ecology.

For centuries the Prince Bishops of Durham have been very much in evidence throughout the upper reaches of the Wear. They owned the land and leased the region's rich coal and lead mines for considerable profit. On the south banks of the Killhope Burn is the Killhope Lead Mine which is Britain's best preserved lead mining site. The Romans mined the lead in Weardale and during the Middle Ages lead was used by the Prince Bishops for the roof of Durham Cathedral. The present chapel in St John's Chapel was built on a small 'chapel of ease' that was used by the Prince Bishops when they were out hunting. The nearby Westgate and Eastgate mark the boundaries of a large deer hunting park that they created in the thirteenth century. Frosterley 'marble', a decorative limestone, was used by them to decorate the Chapel of Nine Altars in Durham Cathedral and at Wolsingham, in 1341, a Bishop's manor house was built, as was a rectory, for the use of their hunting guests.

Bishop Auckland is the official residence of the present Bishop of Durham and has been the Bishops' principal residence since the twelfth century. Auckland Castle was converted from a manor house by Bishop Bek around 1300. From Norman times, until 1836 when their powers were finally returned to the Crown, the Prince Bishops of Durham ruled over a huge area that stretched from the south bank of the Tyne to the Tees. The Prince Bishops' Norman Cathedral and Castle still dominate the medieval city of Durham.

Dere Street, the Roman Road, crossed the Wear north of Bishop Auckland near the remains of Binchester Roman Fort, which contains Britain's best example of a military bath-suite. The not-far-away Saxon church at Escomb, the oldest and most complete Anglo-Saxon church in Britain, is largely built of stone taken from Binchester Fort.

A few kilometres north of Durham, situated on the north banks of the Wear, is Chester-le-Street, once a Roman station situated halfway between Binchester and the Roman Bridge that crossed the River Tyne at Newcastle. Chester-le-Street was where the Lindisfarne monks, when fleeing from the Vikings, kept the body of St Cuthbert before he was finally laid to rest at Durham Cathedral.

After Chester-le-Street the river passes Fatfield and Washington New Town on its north bank before passing under the Wearmouth Bridges through the City of Sunderland and the lower estuary which, over the centuries, was straightened, deepened and protected, to finally arrive at the sea – a journey of some 109km.

Stanhope Village Churchyard. The inscription reads: "This column is all that remains of the Market Cross erected on the occasion of the re-founding of Stanhope Market in 1669 by Bishop John Cosin."

Killhope Burn Lead Mine – Britain's best preserved lead mining site.

CHAPTER ONE

IBERIAN TO CELT: pre-Roman tribal origins
(c. 10,000BC-55BC)

Before the Roman occupation of Britain, just after the birth of Christ, over nine tenths of the total length of time of human occupation in Britain had already taken place. 'Pre-history' is the name often given to this long period before the Roman occupation, the time when historians rely heavily on archaeology (as they do in early Anglo-Saxon times) and when giving a date to any specific event or series of events is difficult. Pre-history evolved slowly, over thousands of years, and although dates and 'ages' are given in this chapter they are included for guidance only. Cultural and technological changes did not occur instantly or widely – they evolved at markedly different rates and geographical locations. For example, by 700BC the Iron Age was well advanced in Central Europe (present day Austria) but iron technology did not arrive in the Outer Hebrides, Scotland until c. 600AD, over a thousand years later.

To understand the cultural and tribal origins of the people of the North East it is necessary to return some ten thousand years to the last glaciers of the Pleistocene epoch of the Ice Age, an epoch that had already lasted some one and a half million years. When the ice melted, around 8,000BC, modern man (Homo sapiens) had already evolved and Continental Europe and Britain were joined at the Sussex Downs. As ice turned to water throughout Britain, a land previously scraped clean by glaciers, North European flowers gradually began to blossom and new forests sprang up – juniper, birch and later pine – eventually to grow in such profusion as to make much of the island impenetrable. The forests and coastal plains became home to myriads of birds and large and small wild animals. Deer were plentiful and much sought after by the early hunters who were moving north following the melting glaciers. No doubt many of these middle to late Stone Age hunters were stranded when the sea level rose, first cutting away Ireland, by the Irish Sea, and then the continent by the English Channel.

The new forests and undergrowth continued to grow thicker, darker and uninterrupted over the uplands and lowlands and the skin-clad hunters were forced to live in the water-logged valleys and coastal regions. They settled on lightly forested or barren highlands, around the marshes of the fenlands and on the coastal plains. The mountains of North Wales, the Pennine range and the Scottish Highlands were inhospitable but later became a refuge from the continental invaders, the Celts, Romans, Anglo-Saxons and Vikings who were to sweep through the southern and eastern lowlands of Britain for almost a thousand years.

2,000BC

In time the flint-tipped tools and spears of these early nomadic hunters became increasingly sophisticated. They started to settle and live together in bands, creating farmsteads in clearings near a water source. They became shepherds, they domesticated animals and developed metal-working skills that were probably imported from the European continent. They raised huge monuments such as Stonehenge, and their country was not isolated from the rest of the world. Ships and men from the countries of the Mediterranean and the European continent were abroad and trading with this northern island.

Mediterranean sea trade began at least around 3,000BC. One of the earliest records of sea trade was when Pharaoh Sneferu of Egypt (2,613-2,589BC) sent 40 ships to Phoenicia to bring back cedar wood from the forests of Lebanon. The Egyptians were then a powerful trading nation exchanging goods with the Phoenicians and Syrians. When ancient Egyptian civilisation declined the Phoenicians (whose major cities – Tyre, Sidon and Byblos – were all ports) became the most powerful trading nation in the Mediterranean. Phoenicia had natural harbours situated along the present day Syrian coast which were strategically placed on the caravan routes from the wealthy inland empires of Cathay, Persia and Babylonia. They acted as middle-men for trade to the western Mediterranean, North Africa and down the Red Sea. Their ships sailed through the Straits of Gibraltar, along the Iberian coast and up to Britain – there were jade, gold and pearls in plenty in this remote northern island. Egyptian beads were brought to Britain c. 1,200BC, and British jet, perhaps from the North East of England, was carried to Spain c. 2,500BC.

The Phoenicians were the dominant seafarers for well over a thousand years, developing trade through much of the world – even sailing clockwise round Africa. Then in 332BC Alexander the Great sacked Tyre, slew most of the inhabitants and started the Macedonian-Greek empire's rise to supremacy. But it was not to last for long; soon the mighty Romans were to become masters of the Mediterranean Sea and extend sea trade as far north as Britain.

The Eltingham Flint. The blade, found on the boulder clay of the valley, pushes the known human presence in the Tyne Valley back into the Palaeolithic period, around 8,000BC.

wood available from the extensive forests to build huts and to fuel the open fires that smelted the copper and tin of the Bronze Age. In Cornwall the local tribesmen became skilled bronze workers as copper and tin were plentiful and the ores close to the surface. The wheel and the plough were independently and simultaneously invented in Eurasia and many other places, and throughout Bronze Age Britain agriculture continued to develop.

The Bronze Age of Central Europe commenced around 1,200BC. The Bronze Age was followed by the Iron Age. For example, around 700BC in present day Austria, an advanced group of early Iron Age cultures (the so-called 'Urnfield' people who buried their cremated dead in pottery urns) exported beautifully made and decorated iron swords.

The people who occupied a large part of continental Europe in the Iron Age were known as the Celts and their origins date back to around 1200BC, the beginning of the Bronze Age. There were many Celtic tribes each with their chiefs and a warrior aristocracy. Druid priests, who conducted human sacrifices, educated the young aristocracy. The Celts had elaborate burial rituals involving first wagons and later chariots. They are rightly famous for the development of their beautiful and characteristic curvilinear designs.

Trade and empire building mixes races and results in technological and cultural change. The Phoenician trading route to Britain followed the coast of southern and eastern Spain which was home, from at least 1,000BC, to the Iberians who were skilled metal-workers, miners and farmers. When the Bronze Age came to Britain, the technologies of the local British tribes were probably much enhanced by Iberian skills. Gradually the Iberians lost their cultural identity, first to the Celts and later to Roman expansionism.

1,200BC

The early British artisans slowly developed their primitive, pre-Celtic civilisation and the island's population increased. There was much

700-500BC

From about 700BC the British Iron Age evolved along similar lines to that of Continental Europe. The British Celts built lightly-constructed houses of timber, wattle and mud and, although much of the land was still heavily forested, grew crops: wheat in the south and oats in the north. They hunted, gathered, domesticated animals (dog, pig, oxen, horse), cleared the land, tilled the soil to make permanent fields and fought each other. They worked iron skilfully, and there were significant iron deposits to be found in Britain: some in the Sussex Weald, more in the then-unexploited North – its time was yet to come. Hill forts were built and sometimes villages with small enclosures sprang up. The Celtic tribes may have been ruled by kings with a warrior aristocracy and powerful priesthood but much of Celtic society was made up of farmers.

It is not yet clear why there was parallel evolution of the Iron Age in the island of Britain and Continental Europe. It could have been through successive Continental Celtic tribal invasions through the beaches and lowlands of south and east Britain; or there may have been a series of powerful Celtic chiefs who conquered Britain and then returned to fight and conquer the continental tribes; or perhaps the Celtic culture was peacefully brought to Britain through trade. It could well have been a complex mix of all three. The British and Continental tribes did fight each other, first with bronze and later with iron weapons, and by the time the Romans arrived in Britain, under Caesar, the British Celtic tribes were similar to the Celts of Continental Europe.

The many Celtic tribes that arrived in Continental Europe and Britain from about 700BC probably had common genes – they were tall, red-haired and fair-skinned. Perhaps the more militant and powerful Celtic tribes drove the weaker tribes north and west, to the mountain refuges of Wales, Cornwall and Scotland. Today the people of Wales, Ireland and Scotland are often said to be people of 'Celtic' origin while those of southern and eastern England are considered to be of 'Anglo-Saxon' lineage but this is likely to be an over-simplification. The northern Welsh, a supposedly pure 'Celtic race', are small and dark. The mountains of the north and west of Britain were probably a final refuge for some Celtic clans but they were perhaps also the isolated homes of the early Britons.

200BC

Some of the British Celtic tribes created relatively large settlements (Colchester for example), developing their own monetary

Harpoon of deerhorn found near the coast between Tynemouth and Wearmouth at Whitburn. Dated to be from c. 6,000BC.

A Bronze Age urn used to preserve the ashes of the cremated dead. It was found at Ryton on the River Tyne.

system and maintaining regular contact with their kinsmen abroad, notably the Continental 'Belgae'. Some of the southern Celtic tribes adopted the Belgic culture and perhaps even supplied men to fight alongside their kinsmen against the Romans in northern Gaul. In southern Britain the rich Celtic culture flourished, especially their beautiful metalwork and pottery.

Thus Celtic art, culture and tradition had a marked influence on pre-Roman Britain, but it was much diminished following the Roman invasion of Britain in 43AD. By 200BC the Roman Empire had become so powerful that it brought peace and stability to the shores of the Mediterranean, even controlling sea trade in the Black Sea and Indian Ocean. By 100BC Roman military might and expansionism had much reduced the Celtic cultural influence throughout Continental Europe.

Two Rivers

10,000BC

The Rivers Trent and Ouse and the wide Humber estuary, which is their outlet into the North Sea, for centuries acted as natural barriers between the immediate 'South', the flat fertile lands of Lincolnshire and the Fens, and the 'North', the moorlands and forests of Yorkshire and Durham that lead up to the next significant, natural barrier on the East coast – the River Tyne. But it is likely that the Humber barrier was crossed by early man.

The Tyne and the Wear were ice-bound through much of the Palaeolithic Age and far from the southern entry points into Britain. From about 8,000BC onwards the climate must have been most inhospitable to the few hunters who crossed the Humber to come north to the banks of the Tyne and Wear.

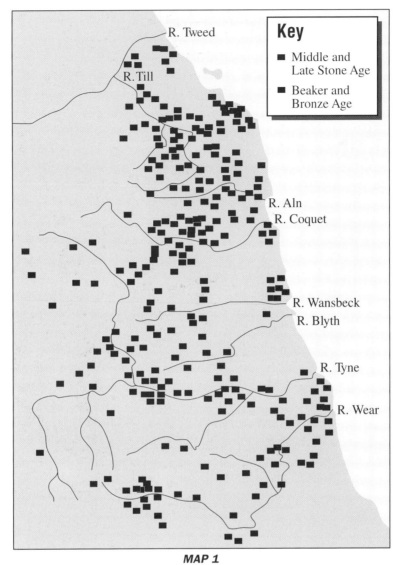

R. Tweed

R. Till

Key
■ Middle and
  Late Stone Age
■ Beaker and
  Bronze Age

R. Aln
R. Coquet

R. Wansbeck
R. Blyth

R. Tyne

R. Wear

MAP 1
*Settlements and finds from the Bronze and Stone Ages showing how they
tend to be located on the river valleys and coastal plains.*

5,000BC (Middle Stone Age)

There is evidence of settlers in the North East region during the Mesolithic period, the middle division of the Stone Age around 5,000BC, when temperatures rose some three degrees Centigrade above present day. During the Mesolithic period very small stone tools were produced with wooden, bone or antler handles and fragments of these small stone tools (microliths) have been found around the more accessible valleys and coastal flats of the North East (see Map 1 above). The forests were becoming deciduous but remained virtually impregnable to the lightweight tools of the men of the Middle Stone Age. The waterlogged valleys of the Tyne and Wear were used by these early settlers to follow the summer time migrations of the herds of deer as they moved to the uplands in search of grazing. During summer and autumn shellfish, sea fish and salmon, returning in their thousands to the rivers to spawn, must have made a welcome addition to their diet.

c. 3,500BC (Late Stone Age)

The Neolithic period (c. 3500BC, the final division of the Stone Age) followed the Mesolithic period and is characterised by the appearance of the earliest settled agricultural communities and man learning to grind and flake stone to make increasingly sophisticated tools. The North East's Neolithic settlers, with their heavier, more sophisticated tools, started to clear forests. They tended livestock, hunted, gathered and built religious monuments. They buried their dead in round cairns and long earthen mounds, barrows, and raised stone circles to their gods.

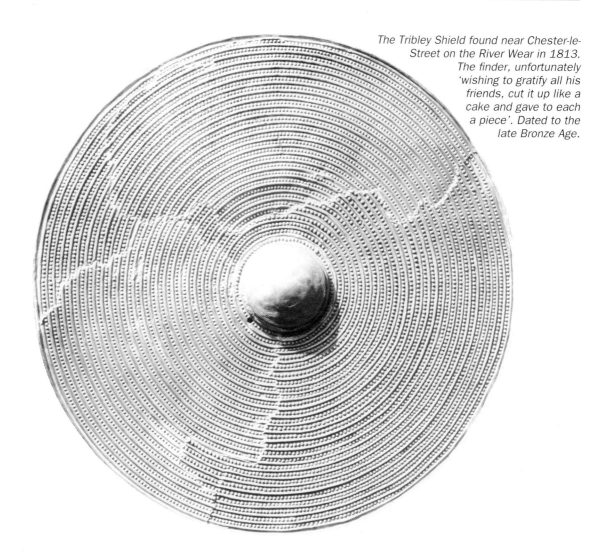

The Tribley Shield found near Chester-le-Street on the River Wear in 1813. The finder, unfortunately 'wishing to gratify all his friends, cut it up like a cake and gave to each a piece'. Dated to the late Bronze Age.

The log boat found in 1885 near the ferry crossing of the Wear at Hylton and estimated to be from around 2,000BC.

Iron Age settlement.

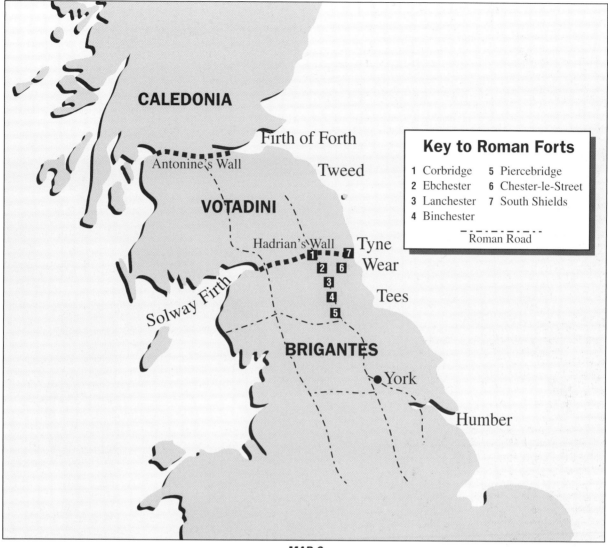

MAP 2
The Celtic and Roman North East.

c. 1700BC (Bronze Age)

Around 1700BC the 'Beaker people', thus named because they buried their dead in stone cists in round barrows along with characteristic short-necked, beaker-like pottery, were evident in the region (Hastings Hill, Sunderland, for example). It is not clear if the 'Beaker people' were an actual tribe or an absorbed beaker culture (like the Urnfield people, see page 7) that originated in Continental Europe. From c. 1,000BC the people of the North East cremated rather than inhumed (placing of the body in a cist) their dead.

An extremely important late Bronze Age find was made in the North East at Heathery Burn Cave near Stanhope on the River Wear. Amongst a mass of spear heads, ornaments, a sheet-bronze bucket and utensils, was one of the earliest finds of a wheel in Britain. Another find on the Wear was a log boat estimated to be

from around 2,000BC and recovered from the bed of river near the ancient ferry crossing at Hylton in 1885. It is Sunderland's earliest known boat!

c. 600BC (Iron Age)

Probably during the Iron Age, perhaps from about 600BC, Celtic tribes and culture began to influence the region and perhaps displace the local clans. Iron Age settlers continued to clear the forests, especially in the middle Wear valley, and farm the land in scattered undefended settlements made up of a few lightly built huts surrounded by wooden stake fences contained within an enclosure that was perhaps home to a few domesticated animals – sheep, cattle and horses. They cremated their dead (hence the lack of burial sites) and constructed 'hill forts'. These defensive sites were not always built on hills and were not necessarily forts – possibly status symbols for the local chiefs. They were built first of wood and turf, but later the defences were made of stone although the huts were still of wood. Remnants have been found on coastal headlands as well as on the river valley hilltops.

By the time of the Roman invasion the North East was dominated by the fierce Celtic tribe the Brigantes ('upland people'), who ruled the land between the Humber estuary and the Tyne or even north of the Tyne to mid-Northumberland. Further north around the Cheviots were the numerous hill forts of the Votadini tribe and north of them were the partly Celtic, but equally fierce, Caledonians (Map 2). The Romans largely, but not completely, ignored these Celtic defensive sites, preferring to build a completely new infrastructure based on a network of roads connecting forts garrisoned by auxiliary units – a well tried and extremely effective means of controlling a conquered population.

The Roman roads were for trade as well as troops. The city of Rome depended on trade for its survival and sea transport played

an important role: it was cheaper to sail cargo from one end of the Roman Empire to the other than to transport it 100 miles overland. It was not long after the Roman legions marched north that Roman ships were entering the River Tyne. The Tyne was to become the northernmost river and limit of their mighty Empire and the river was soon to have its first important sea port at present-day South Shields.

Above: Late Bronze Age sword from the River Tyne.

Right: Bronze Age spearhead from the River Tyne. It was probably thrown into the river to fulfil a vow or as an offering, or perhaps lost on a hunting expedition.

CHAPTER TWO

THE ROMAN INVASION: Julius Caesar to the Wall (55BC-AD300)

J ulius Caesar revitalised and extended a declining Roman Empire and, through his tactics, fighting skill and uncanny ability to lead both legionaries and the Senate, extended Roman influence into northern Europe. He made France, at least, a permanently Latin country and ensured that Rome was to influence Europe for at least another 500 years (1500 in the near Middle East). In 55BC he led a small expeditionary force across the Dover Straits and a year later returned with a larger force. He crossed the Thames and won several battles, showing the Celtic tribes that their screaming hordes led by their chiefs in chariots were no match for his disciplined, battle-winning legionaries.

AD43

Caesar conquered Gaul but he did not conquer Britain. This followed some one hundred eventful years later, 43 years after the birth of Christ, and the conqueror was Emperor Claudius. Claudius probably needed a great victory to make himself popular in Rome and, once conquered, Britain was of little interest. The country, like all Roman provinces, was left in the hands of governors. Some southern Celtic tribes were already seduced by the power, might and luxury of Imperial Rome before Claudius arrived and Celts were already trading and settling in southern Britain from Roman Gaul. There was little resistance from the almost-Romanised, southern British Celts when Claudius' invasion came, but the

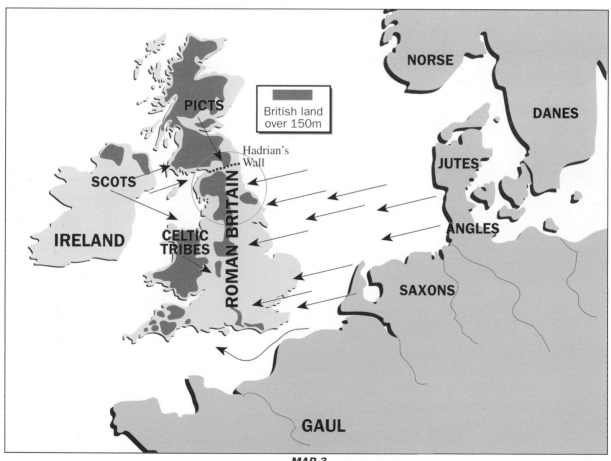

MAP 3
The tribal violation of Roman Britain.

Hadrian's Wall at Housesteads Roman Fort, looking east.

Scotland and Northern Ireland and is said to have been much admired by his contemporaries when he successfully ordered his fleet to sail round Britain. His aim was, as always with Roman generals, to destroy the enemy so completely that all their land was surrendered to the Roman Emperor who was in overall command of the legions.

The Romans built large bases called fortresses as well as smaller forts. They connected their fortresses and forts with a superb network of roads: the legionaries were not only skilled masons and road builders but also well-trained and well-equipped infantrymen. Agricola pressed his legions north and had a victory over the northern Caledonian tribes in AD84 at 'Mons Graupius', possibly at the foot of the Scottish Highlands. But although he subdued the North of England he and the Romans never conquered the Scots. They mounted expeditions, a serious one in AD130, but the Scottish terrain was always too difficult, the Roman lines of communication too stretched and the legions were often withdrawn because of continental rebellions.

Hadrian was Roman Emperor from AD117 to 138 and spent much of his reign touring the Empire. To define the northern limit of the province of Britain, as part of his generally defensive foreign policy, he ordered the building of Hadrian's Wall. It was built between AD122-128 and Hadrian was perhaps inspired by travellers describing the Great Wall of China.

In AD210 Emperor Severus decided to annex Scotland but failed. He renovated Emperor Hadrian's Wall which had previously been breached by the Picts. When the Romans came to the North East the region had already been inhabited for thousands of years: the Romans stayed for three hundred and then most of them left, leaving behind a superb system of roads. They colonised modern England and Wales, building villas and some fine walled cities, notably York and London, and especially Romanising and introducing Christianity to the lowlands of South and East England. Following the birth of Christ, and

legionaries met stiff resistance when they arrived at the foot of the Welsh mountains, when they crossed the Humber or later when they pushed into the south west under Emperor Vespasian. It took more than ten years of fierce fighting to overcome the anti-Roman faction of the Brigantes of the North.

AD80

Julius Agricola (AD40-93) was a Roman general who after fighting with the legions in Britain was sent there as governor in AD78. He remained governor until AD84 (when he was recalled to Rome) and during his rule followed a policy of continued Romanisation in the South and conquest, expansion and exploration in the North. Under his command the Roman legions, around 5,000 men per legion, first arrived on the banks of the Tyne in the AD80s. He pushed his legions into

Pons Aelius.

through the missionary activity of St Paul, Christianity spread rapidly throughout the Roman Empire despite the attempts of various Emperors to stamp it out. The Romans had less success in the North and West where pagan Celtic tribalism was never really overcome and Scotland remained unconquered.

The legions did not immediately depart from Britain. There was rather a slow collapse that began in AD410. Honorius the Roman emperor, much threatened by the breakdown of the Rhine frontier in AD406, told the Romano-British settlements that he was unable to supply any more troops to the island and it had thus to fend for itself. Many legionaries had already left Britain to fight on the Rhine front, leaving behind many peaceful, unprotected Romano-British settlements, especially in the South and East. As and when the Romans departed the Celtic tribes from North Wales and West England broke out of their mountain refuges to attack the undefended settlements which were also an easy prey for German tribes, the Jutes, Angles and Saxons, who sailed in from the North Sea to attack and settle the undefended coasts. The Scots crossed the Irish Sea to join in the plunder as did the Picts and northern tribes who swept down from the North through the abandoned Hadrian's Wall (Map 3, page 15).

The Romans left many remains – roads, villas, forts, walls – but their long term influence on Britain was never as great as that of the countries of the North Sea rim. Britain was never as Latinised as France but it was lastingly affected by the following centuries of Germanic and Scandinavian invasions.

Two Rivers

AD80

The Romans arrived in the North under the command of Julius Agricola in the AD80s and they consolidated their position along the Tyne-Solway gap before pushing north into Scotland and built a series of bridges, fords, roads, forts and camps to create a pattern of settlement that is the basis of many of the North East's modern towns and villages. Agricola built the forts at Corbridge and Carlisle and the road that links them, the Stanegate. They also probably built the stone arched bridge at Corbridge to carry Dere

Street, the main supply route up from York, one of the key Roman cities and military fortresses. Some distance away from the modern town of Corbridge the remains of the Roman bridge have been unearthed. When the bridge collapsed in the fifth or sixth century the Corbridge settlement may have moved closer to a shallower, more fordable spot on the Tyne as perhaps the inhabitants were unable to repair or rebuild the bridge as Roman bridge building technology was long forgotten. The original bridge was probably elaborate and decorative with a ramp, statues, a balustrade and possibly even approached through triumphal arches.

Altar from the River Tyne at Newcastle, dedicated to the god Neptune. This formed one of a pair from a shrine on the Roman Bridge, Pons Aelius, over the river, the other being dedicated to Oceanus, the sea god. It is likely that it is Neptune's role as a god of fresh water which is being invoked as the bridge was close to the point where the tidal sea water met the Tyne waters.

Above:
Sestertius of Hadrian from the River Tyne at the site of the Roman Bridge, Newcastle, AD132-4. The Emperor Hadrian appears as a victorious commander with the legend HADRIANUS AUGUSTUS – 'Hadrian Emperor'. Possibly a votive offering to the river.

Below:
Reverse of the sestertius of Hadrian showing the emperor on the imperial barge with a wind god as a figurehead on the prow. The legend reads FELICITATI AUG(USTI) CO(N)S(ULIS) III P(ATRIS) P(ATRIAE) – 'For the good fortune of the emperor, thrice consul, father of his country'. The 'SC' indicates that the coin was minted on the orders of the Senate.

Left:
Roman ship with triangular topsail (from Torr, 1894).

Below:
Model of a Roman merchant ship, c. AD200, which could have been used to bring troops and/or grain to the Tyne.

AD120

Emperor Hadrian built his famous wall along the Tyne-Solway gap, possibly 'to keep out the barbarians' and define the northern limit of the Empire. It was built by the IInd, VIth and XXth legions; ten feet wide, some fifteen feet high, and constructed partly of stone and partly of turf. It was not long before the turf wall sector was replaced with stone. When finished the wall had 16 major forts, a number of smaller forts (milecastles) and a system of watch towers/signalling stations. The milecastles protected gates that were based at intervals of a Roman mile (1000 paces) right along the Wall's 85-mile length. The eastern end was first terminated at a narrow point on the Tyne (near the mouth of a small stream, the Lort Burn) so as to build a bridge across the Tyne.

The Tyne at Newcastle was then a shallower, wider river and the Romans spanned it with a magnificent stone bridge – perhaps over 700ft long and some 20ft wide. Its walkway, probably made of wood, was supported by stone piers each with an upstream and downstream cutwater. It was called Pons Aelius, or the Aelian Bridge since 'Aelius' was Emperor Hadrian's family name. The bridge was probably sited near the present day Swing Bridge. This is thought to be the site because a large number of Roman artifacts were discovered there during the building of the Swing Bridge. A shrine was set up on the completed bridge in AD123 by the (Roman) VIth legion which sailed from Germany to reinforce and work with the existing legions. They dedicated the shrine to the sea-gods Neptune and Oceanus, perhaps to give thanks for their safe passage across the North Sea. The foundations and cutwaters of Pons Aelius may have been used by the Normans when they built their bridge over the Tyne following the Conquest (see page 45). It is possible that the Roman bridge, or at least a good part of it, might have lasted some 1000 years.

To protect the bridge and a little harbour in the Tyne off Lort Burn the Romans built a fort on the north bank of the river. The fort took its name from the bridge and was eventually to become the site of a Norman castle and the city of Newcastle upon Tyne. There are a few existing remains of the Roman fort.

While the Wall was being constructed it was decided to extend it eastwards to Wallsend (Segedunum) to prevent the Wall from being flanked. Major forts were built at Benwell (Condercum), at Rudchester (Vindbola), north of present day Wylam, and at Halton (Hunnum). The fort at Corbridge (Corstopitum), built near the Roman bridge and Dere Street, played an important military role in the occupation of northern Britain as an arsenal and supply base.

The Wall passed north of Corbridge and crossed the North Tyne near a fort on the west bank of the river at Chesters (Cilurnum), just downstream of the present bridge at Chollerford. The three Roman bridges across the Tyne, Chesters, Corbridge and Pons Aelius, probably did not have stone arches, their roadways instead carried on timber beams supported by the stone piers. From Chesters the Wall was taken to Fort Carrawburgh (Brocolitia) and to another fort at Housesteads (Vercovicium). At Housesteads a beautiful sculpture of a reclining Neptune was found. Neptune, in addition to being a Roman sea god, was also the god of flowing water – springs, streams and fountains. Chesters and Housesteads are the best preserved of all the 16 forts that stretched along the Tyne-Solway gap.

The Wall was wide enough to have a walkway and it is likely that the soldiers were protected by a simple chest-high parapet. There was a V-shaped ditch in front of the Wall but the Romans never intended it to be a defensive, fighting platform. Roman soldiers fought on foot and would probably advance out of the milecastle gates in the Wall to attack a foe in the field, perhaps forcing them to make a final stand with their backs against the north face of the Wall. Some forts even had cavalry units such as the fort at Chesters. At first the Roman soldiers were housed in garrisons some distance behind the Wall to be called out in times of strife. Later the garrisons were brought up to the Wall and a flat bottomed ditch, the Vallum, was dug behind the Wall with banks on both sides and crossed by causeways at the forts. By garrisoning the Wall and digging the Vallum, the Romans emphasised the Wall's main function which was to act as a barrier, almost like a modern day customs barrier. It was also an observation post as well as a boundary marker of the Roman Empire.

The Romans needed to supply the Tyne valley settlements and Wall forts with men, food and arms. The excellent road system was

Binchester Roman Fort on the River Wear. It is Britain's best example of a military bath suite.

one means but both the sea and the river played important roles. A fort/port was built at the mouth of the Tyne on The Lawe of present day South Shields, possibly by Agricola. Emperor Hadrian definitely built a fort (Arbeia) there and at some time riverside quays must have been constructed, as the Romans' military campaigns relied heavily on sea transport for support. The fort was also used as a grain store perhaps for the forts of the Tyne valley. Arbeia was garrisoned by the Fifth Cohort of Gauls, but during the fourth century they were replaced by a naval force 'numerus barcarri Tigrisiensium', an elite unit of Tigris lightermen (from around Barcarion). The Tigris lightermen may have built barges to carry cargo from the quays at South Shields to the forts along the Tyne – forerunners of the later coal-carrying keel boats which carried coal down the Tyne to ships anchored at the river mouth.

AD200

Hadrian's successor Antoninus Pius (Emperor, AD138-61) pushed about 100 miles north into Scotland from Hadrian's Wall and built the Antonine Wall. This wall was modelled on Hadrian's but built of turf and stretched from the Forth to the Clyde. It was abandoned around AD160 when the Romans pulled back to Hadrian's Wall which was further strengthened and modified. The Military Way was a road built behind the Wall and many of the milecastle gateways were filled in or narrowed. The Vallum was abandoned around AD140, presumably because of Antoninus' Wall. It is also likely that following the Roman style of seducing a conquered population by offering Roman life, luxury and positions of power to the defeated local chieftains, the anti-Roman faction of the Brigantes gradually became less hostile as they were assimilated into Roman Britain.

The origins of the name of the Tyne are obscure but it is possible that the Romans may have called it 'Tinea'. However a map of Britain drawn by Ptolemy c. AD100, shows a northern river labelled 'Verda' but it is unclear if the river is the Tyne or the Wear. The Reverend John Brand in his *History of Newcastle* (1789) wrote: *'the present appellation of this river is implied in the first accounts of a religious house at Tinmouth, evidently so called from its vicinity to the mouth of the Tyne, which was first erected a little after the beginning of the seventh century.'*

However, few would nowadays consider the Reverend Brand as the primary source for the origins of the name of the Tyne!

The Tyne-Solway gap, the narrowness of Britain at this point, the inhospitable land to the north, the depth and width of the River Tyne, which acted both as a barrier and a routeway, all meant that physical geography played a key role in the location of Hadrian's Wall at the frontier of the Roman Empire. The Roman occupation of the Tyne valley ensured that this river and its bridges, villages and towns were to play an early part in the evolution of Britain and the North East. The River Wear, less strategically placed, was to wait until some Anglo-Saxon monks discovered a highly defensible meander loop and built a church. That place was to become the home of the Prince Bishops and the site of the magnificent Durham Cathedral.

Bronze helmet cheekpiece, AD100-200, found in the River Tyne at South Shields. The decoration of punched dots shows one of the Dioscuri, the heavenly twins, either Castor or Pollux. The other cheekpiece will have depicted the other Dioscurus.

CHAPTER THREE

THE NORTH SEA RIM INVASIONS:
Anglo-Saxons and Vikings (c. 300-1000)

For a period of some 700 years, from c. AD300 until just before the Norman Conquest, Britain was again subject to a series of invasions. This time it was the tribes from the countries of the North Sea rim; the Flemish Lowlands, Northern Germany and modern Denmark and Norway. The invasions were to have a marked and continued influence on the British race and history, even more than the Roman invasions, for Britain was never really Latinised as was France. The invading tribes, at first the Angles, Saxons and Jutes, later, Danes and Norsemen (the Vikings), were fierce fighters. The tribes had common root languages, they were loyal to their chiefs or kings, they had many shared gods (like Thor and Woden) and they enjoyed similar epic poetry.

It is possible that some German tribes were already in Britain (serving as mercenaries) during the time of the Romans and perhaps, after the legions left, they rebelled and attacked their defenceless British hosts. The first Saxon raids on Britain were around AD300 and some hundred years later they were arriving in force. The Angles and Saxons attacked and settled in the south and east of Britain. They moved west to Devon and the Angles made inroads into Northumbria. The Jutes attacked and settled in Kent and the Isle of Wight. (There were few racial differences between the Angles and Saxons and some authorities talk of the Anglo-Saxon invasions, although Bede, writing in his *Ecclesiastical History of the English People*, c. 731, separates the invaders into Angles and Saxons as well as Jutes.) Celtic chiefs, courted and Romanised by their overlords, were easy prey in the South and on the eastern seaboard but less so in the more difficult terrain of the

MAP 4
Anglo-Saxon England c. AD600.

North and West, which the Romans never conquered and where British tribalism continued to exist. During the fourth, fifth and sixth centuries the Germanic tribes settled, raided, plundered, slew and fought the Romano-British and the unconquered British tribes. They told heroic stories of their mighty deeds but left no written records – the Germanic tribes were largely illiterate.

When attacking Britain, the Anglo-Saxon warriors, led by an autocratic chief or king, would seek out an estuary, sail their ships up-

St Aidan, Holy Island.

river, land and drive back any existing settlers. If the terrain was suitable they created riverside settlements and then brought over the farmers and the women – the Anglo-Saxons were farmers as well as warriors. They were loyal to chief and kin and Anglo-Saxon settlements were often made up of a small kin-group, perhaps consisting of wooden houses built round a central chief's hall. They largely ignored the gutted Roman villas, although they may have occupied Roman stone-walled towns. The mainly unprotected villas and Romano-British settlements were also easy targets for the Picts who streamed south across the defunct Hadrian's Wall to attack the undefended villas, towns and cities. Fierce Irish tribes known as the 'Scots' came in from the West to enjoy the plunder and the Anglo-Saxon invaders either clashed or joined forces with the Picts and Scots as the 'barbarian tribes' fought over the remains of civilised, Christian, Romano-Britain (Map 3, page 15). Life in Roman-British villas and towns first deteriorated, then died.

Roman Christianity declined or died in the East as the pagan Anglo-Saxons conquered the British tribes. At one time, according to Bede, a whole nation of Angles left lower Denmark, the land between the kingdoms of the Jutes and Saxons, to settle in 'Angleland' or England. Throughout the whole of the fifth and sixth centuries the Angles, Saxons and

Jutes continued to invade and settle along the eastern and southern coast of Britain such that, over the centuries, the Anglo-Saxon conquests developed into a series of kingdoms that stretched from the Firth of Forth to West Devon – from Northumbria to Wessex. The Romano-British were pushed westwards and forced along with the British tribes into enclaves in South West England, Wales, North West England and South West Scotland (Map 4, page 24). By about AD600 the British tribes were more or less decimated apart from a few isolated regions: Cornwall was to remain a Celtic enclave until the ninth century.

Despite the pagan, Anglo-Saxon invasions, Christianity returned to Britain: from Ireland in the North and Rome in the South. St Patrick (c. 390-60), a Romanised Briton, was captured at the age of 16 in West England by a marauding band of Irish (Scots) and held captive in Ireland until he escaped to Gaul. He later returned to Ireland as a missionary and by the time of his death had converted much of Ireland's mutually hostile Celtic tribes to Christianity. The Christian monasteries of Ireland were to play a key role in bringing back Christianity to Britain, especially to Scotland and Northumbria, through such dedicated monks as St Columba and St Aidan. St Columba (c. 521-597), an Irish Scot, founded the monastery on Iona off the west coast of

The southern entrance to the seventh century, stone Escomb church, County Durham. A rare example of an intact Anglo-Saxon church since most Anglo-Saxon churches were constructed of wood and have not survived.

and Latin scholar, he did much to bring about the gradual spread of Christianity throughout Britain. Churches were built, simple rectangular buildings with perhaps a nave for the worshippers and a square chancel at the east end for the priest. The traditional 'parish system' began to take root where a settlement was attached to its own church and clergyman. Although during Anglo-Saxon times there was no clear distinction between Church and State, the seeds were sown where 'Church' and 'State' could be represented by bishop and king, priest and landowner or thegn (a thegn later 'thane', was a 'lesser noble', a member of a class between earl and freeman).

Scotland. From there mainland Scotland and its many Celtic tribes were evangelised – the Picts of North Scotland and Galloway, the Irish Scots of Argyllshire and the Britons of Strathclyde.

Gregory the Great, Pope from 590-604, lifted the Church of Rome out of a seemingly hopeless situation brought about by the collapse of the Western half of the Roman Empire in the fifth century. He strengthened the Church of Rome, had great success in limiting Imperial authority over the Church and, in 596, sent a Roman monk Augustine to Kent to convert the Anglo-Saxons to Christianity. Augustine converted Ethelbert I of Kent, a task made easier since his Frankish wife was already a Christian. Augustine founded the See of Canterbury and created there a centre of Christianity. He antagonised the Celtic Welsh Christians at a conference on the banks of the River Severn. Roman Christianity spread slowly beyond Canterbury. The first important success in the North was in the kingdom of Northumbria with the conversion of King Edwin and the Northumbrians to the Roman Church.

The Roman Church further developed its power and influence in Anglo-Saxon England when in 669 Rome appointed Theodore, a Greek from Tarsus, to be Archbishop of Canterbury. An extremely able man and a Greek

No sooner had the Anglo-Saxon invaders settled down to a reasonably civilised, Christian way of life than the next wave of North Sea rim invasions started. This time it was the Vikings, races similar to the Anglo-Saxons, perhaps even more independent and fierce, and also pagan. 'Viking' means pirate and was applied by their victims to three Scandinavian races – Norwegians, Danes and Swedes – which by the end of the eighth century had formed nations. People from the oldest nation, Sweden, went east, while those from Norway and Denmark went south and west to Continental Europe and Britain.

At the time of the Viking invasions the Anglo-Saxon kingdoms were divided:

Above Escomb church door is a seventeenth century sundial. The Anglo-Saxon sundial to its right, and shown here, is made up of a beast above a serpent and the three lines could represent three daily times of prayer. The serpent was a creator god for the Angles.

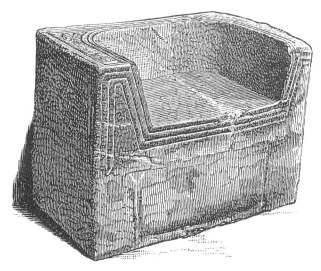

The stone bishop's seat at Hexham Abbey, Northumberland, which is a relic from St Wilfrid's Hexham monastery. Wilfrid (639-709) was a Northumbrian aristocrat who travelled to Rome with Benedict Biscop in 652 (page 35). Wilfrid was loyal to the Roman Church and he converted many Saxons to Christianity in the south of England.

Northumbria's power was gradually declining and its nobility feuded. Mercia fought Northumbria and then Wessex fought Mercia; but there was no overall victor, even though by 825 King Egbert of Wessex had broken much of Mercia's power and Northumbria recognised his overlordship. Britain was a divided island as the Anglo-Saxon dynasties fought each other. Much of Northumbria and all Mercia were conquered by the Vikings; but for Wessex and King Alfred the Great, the Norsemen would have swept right through England.

The first recorded Viking raids took place in the South in 789. They killed the reeve of Dorchester after they landed at Portland. The *Anglo-Saxon Chronicle* records that in that year: '...*came three ships of Norwegians from Horthaland: and then the reeve rode thither and tried to compel them to go to the royal manor, for he did not know what they were: and then they slew him*'.

(A reeve was the king's bailiff, or king's executive in each Anglo-Saxon 'shire'. The 'Shire reeve', which became 'Sheriff', was the king's representative in Shire Courts and also responsible for collecting crown revenue. The Sheriff continued to play this important role for the king as local government evolved over the centuries.)

There were two main Viking sea-routes to Britain: one round the north, via the Shetland and Orkney Islands, to West Scotland, Ireland

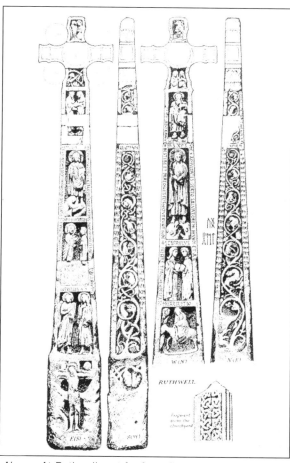

Above: At Ruthwell, not far from Gretna Green, Scotland, is the magnificently carved 5.2 m high, eighth century Ruthwell Cross. The Latin inscriptions and stone carvings on the four sides of the cross describe an old English poem and the religious background of Northumbrian Christianity. (Illustrations by W. G. Collingwood, 1917.)

Below: The Rothbury Cross, Northumberland, discovered in Rothbury Church in 1850. Another Anglo-Saxon stone cross exists at Bewcastle. All three stone crosses (from Ruthwell, Rothbury and Bewcastle) are similar in design and it is likely that they came from the stone carvers of the Northumbrian centres of learning at Wearmouth and Jarrow.

Viking Longship.

and Wales; these were mainly Norwegians, and the other across the North Sea to Eastern and Southern England; these were mainly Danish. The Vikings occupied the Isle of Man and sailed as far south as the Mediterranean and as far north as Iceland, Greenland and eventually across the Atlantic to North America.

The Vikings went to sea in open-decked, clinker-built longships that were similar to those used by their predecessors the Angles, Saxons and Jutes. Between c. AD400 and 1200 the essential characteristics of these ships changed little; the raiding longships were rowed, had a single square sail that was used when the wind was in the right direction and were fast, sleek and manoeuvrable. Their traders, when compared to the longships, were shorter, with wider beams and more rounded hulls and were known as 'knarrs'.

The Norwegian Vikings settled in Ireland, the Shetland and Orkney Islands, the Hebrides and on the Scottish mainland in Sutherland and Caithness. There were easy, rich pickings to be had as the Church had built many of its monasteries on the banks of large navigable rivers or offshore islands, all prime targets for skilled, warrior-mariners. The Lindisfarne monastery in the North East was plundered in 793 and in the following year the Norwegian Vikings entered the Tyne and attacked St Paul's monastery at Jarrow. By 795 the monastery on Iona had been sacked.

A second, ninth century, wave of Viking invasions was Danish. According to the *Anglo-Saxon Chronicle*, the Danes first landed at Sheppey in 835 and for the next 30 years increasingly attacked the settlements along the estuaries and the flat beaches of the eastern seaboard. There was no true Anglo-Saxon fleet and the country was vulnerable to the Vikings who had the ships, the skills and were accomplished pirates and ocean traders. The Danish royal dynasty temporarily fell apart in 854 and, with no uniting force to control them, the warrior-adventurers increased their attacks on England as they spilled out of Denmark to plunder and settle.

In 865 the Danish leaders, Halfdan and Ivar the Boneless, came ashore in East Anglia at the head of the 'Great Army'. They went north to Northumbria and captured York in 867 and in 869 defeated King Edmund of East Anglia. Soon fleets of more than a hundred longships were putting to sea and the Anglo-Saxons succumbed to the bravery and ferocity of the Viking warrior-seamen. The Vikings took horses from East Anglia and, as mounted infantry, the 'Viking host', for five years until 870, rode down the men of Northumbria, East Anglia, Mercia and Wessex. The Anglo-Saxon kingdoms of Northumbria, East Anglia and Mercia became Viking kingdoms. Wessex survived as an Anglo-Saxon kingdom but it was attacked by Guthrum, the Danish King of East Anglia in 878 and his opponent, King Alfred 'the Great,' was forced into hiding in Somerset.

King Alfred 'the Great' of Wessex (871-899) did much to put iron back into the soul of the Anglo-Saxon warriors. He developed a class of mounted fighters to take on the Viking host. At first he was unsuccessful and was forced by the Danes (who had split the 'Great Army' into two with Halfdan going north) to take refuge in the Somerset marshes, from where he fought a successful guerrilla campaign, despite the hostile Welsh at his back. Such was the power of his leadership that he united his thegns and won a decisive battle over King Guthrum at Edington in 878. He allowed the Vikings to keep their conquests in Mercia and East Anglia provided that Guthrum was converted to Christianity and that the Danes retired to the land already held under the Viking/Danish laws (the Danelaw).

Alfred had taken London in 886 and walled and garrisoned it. He secured his position against the Vikings by building a navy with longships larger than the Viking ones, with 60 oars or more, some 30 road-linked, planned fortified towns (burhs), often with regular grids of streets, to control all England south of the Thames. He brought peace to 'Angelcynn'

Viking attack.

(as he called the land of the English people) and realising the dramatic loss of the Northumbrian Christian tradition of art and learning, he developed education and literature in his own kingdom. It is likely that he studied Latin and personally translated Bede's work from Latin into Anglo-Saxon or English. He instigated the recording of the *Anglo-Saxon Chronicle* and a system of administration for his kingdom.

In time Alfred's son, Edward the Elder (899-924), and his son, Athelstan (924-939) reconquered the kingdoms of Mercia and East Anglia, an area which along with the Viking kingdom of York, had become known as the 'Danelaw'. The Danelaw Vikings were slowly converted to Christianity and, like their Anglo-Saxon predecessors, settled down to a peaceful way of life. The Anglo-Saxons built their fortified burhs in the Danelaw, garrisons were constructed at strategic points and the land divided up into 'shires', forerunners of the shires and counties of England.

For much of the tenth century the Vikings left the House of Wessex and the emerging kingdom of England alone. The quiet reign of King Edgar (959-975) was marked by the development of laws and growing unity both between and within the Danelaw and Wessex. The 'Witan' or royal council actively made many laws and charters. Edgar developed a system of English currency that remained in use long after the Norman Conquest and built monasteries which were wealthy and important centres of art and learning.

However the English and the Scandinavians never became a truly united people and, geographically separated, they were easy prey to a second Danish invasion. It came at the end of the tenth century. The Danes, a more disciplined and formidable fighting force than ever and, after a series of raids between 994 and 1002, the English, led by King Ethelred the Unready (968-1016), followed a policy of 'peace at any price' and bought from the Danish Vikings with massive financial payments. To prevent the Danes from raiding out of Normandy Channel ports King Ethelred made a treaty with the Duchy of Normandy, even marrying the Duke's daughter to create the first, fateful, link between Normandy and England. In order to raise the huge sums of 'peace money' he developed a tax and 'Danegeld', as it became known, was the fore-runner of the British tax system.

The Danish King Svein Forkbeard returned to England in 1013 (he had raided in 994) with an army and those in the Danelaw welcomed him. King Ethelred fled to Normandy but later returned. His son Edmund Ironside, in defiance of his father, retook the northern Danelaw including Northumbria. Svein Forkbeard's son Canute (994-1035) fought Edmund Ironside (c. 980-1016) and, on Ironside's death, Canute (or 'Cnut') became King of all England then King of Denmark (1019) and King of Norway (1028). He developed trade between the three countries, which under his kingship became an almost united nation. Canute was tolerant of the Anglo-Saxons, he married Ethelred's widow, and in 1027 he became a Christian. He built monasteries and made a pilgrimage to Rome. At his court both languages, Anglo-Saxon and Danish, were used and he promoted and accepted the Anglo-Saxon rulers of the church. In 1017 he divided his kingdom into the Earldoms of Northumbria, Mercia, East Anglia and Wessex.

Canute died prematurely at the age of 40 in 1035. At his death the Earl of Northumbria, Siward, was a Dane as was the Earl of East Anglia. The most powerful earl was Godwin, the English Earl of Wessex.

Canute's two sons Harold I and Canute II reigned briefly but the Danish royal line ended when Ethelred's son, Edward the Confessor (1042-1066), became king. Soon England was to become, culturally at least, a part of continental Europe and Normandy in particular, its centuries-old link with the countries of the North Sea rim broken forever.

Two Rivers

In the fourth century the Romanised North was not only attacked by the Angles and Saxons but also by Picts and Scots. In AD367 the Picts, Scots and Angles formed an alliance and attacked the Wall, probably helped by discontented 'areani', the Roman scouts and spies positioned north of the wall. The Wall was breached and skirted but the 'invasion' was repulsed by a small Roman army. Pons Aelius was last mentioned in AD400 in a Roman document which detailed all the military outposts. Fifty years later, following the collapse of the Rhine front under the combined assault of many German tribes in 406, the Roman Empire in the West was no more.

Artist's impression of an early medieval settlement at Thirlings in Northumbria. (Illustration: Terry Ball.)

Some of the Hadrian's Wall forts remained occupied. They may have been modified and lived in up to the 400s or even 500s and even occupied by the incoming Angles. The Angles, perhaps arriving in the region as early as AD500, may have landed at riverside sites on the Tyne and Wear. These rivers flowed through the centre of the kingdom of Bernicia, a region which might have once belonged to a Celtic tribe with a chief named Brynaich. By the end of the sixth century there were two 'Anglian' kingdoms in the North, beyond the Humber – Deira and Bernicia. 'Britonic Celtic' kingdoms were Elmet, around present-day Leeds, Strathclyde, Rheged, on the Solway Firth, and Gododdin, a kingdom south and east of the Clyde (Map 4, page 24).

There is some literary evidence that suggests that in 547 a warrior band of Angles, led by Ida the Flame Bearer, sailed from Yorkshire to land on a wide sweep of sandy beach some 50 miles north of the River Tyne. There the Angles built a stronghold on a basalt platform where Bamburgh Castle is today and perhaps the same site as the coastal hill fort of 'Din Guayroi' that was built earlier by the Britons of Brynaich. The *Anglo-Saxon Chronicle* states that:

'In this year (547) Ida assumed the kingdom, from whom arose the royal race of the Northanhymbra, and reigned twelve years, and he built Bebbanburh, which was first enclosed by a hedge, (stockade) and afterwards by a wall (rampart)'. The Angles may have attacked the Britons of Strathclyde and for a period things went badly for the Angles as they were forced back to their coastal forts at Bamburgh and perhaps Holy Island only to be saved by the outbreak of dissension among the Britons.

In the south of the region, settlements along the rivers of the Humber estuary and more generally the East Riding of Yorkshire, was the kingdom of Deira: its centre became the city of York. Deira was probably an older but smaller kingdom than Bernicia. Traditionally, the royal dynasties of Bernicia and Deira were of similar ancestry, each claiming direct descent from the god Woden. According to legend, King Aethelric of Bernicia acquired the kingdom of Deira from King Aelle, the first recorded King of Deira, on Aelle's death-bed. Aethelric's son, Aethelfrith, married Aelle's daughter and reigned over the two kingdoms which became collectively known as 'Northanhymbra'. Aethelfrith 'the Twister' succeeded to the kingdom of Northanhymbra or 'Northumbria' in 592. He was a powerful warrior and expanded Bernicia westwards through the Tyne valley and there is evidence from place names that his kingdom stretched from the Solway to the Mersey. He fought and defeated the Welsh Celts at Chester, c. 607, to cut off the Welsh tribes from their northern compatriots. Just before the battle, according to Bede, he slaughtered British monks who came from the Bangor Iscoed monastery to pray for a victory for the British tribes. He attacked and defeated the Scots of Argyle and took possession of the Scottish Lowlands; his position was threatened only by the Strathclyde Britons.

Aethelfrith's men had similar success against warriors from the British kingdom of Gododdin in a battle that was described by Aneirin, a late sixth century poet from Gododdin (*Votadini* of the Romans). The poem does not mention Aethelfrith but according to the historian F. Stanton it 'yields chronological indications which point with sufficient clearness to his time'. The poet describes how a band of British warriors from Gododdin was destroyed when they attacked Aethelfrith's Northumbria at Catterick or 'Catraeth'. Mynyddawg was the King of Gododdin; it was a truly disastrous attack for the British tribe and the poem describes the tribal rivalry between the Celts and Angles. Written in AD600, it also describes the heroism of the British tribe as well as the method and weapons of the violent and bloody warfare. The importance of king and kinsmen is much evident in the poem.

Wearing a brooch, in the front rank, bearing weapons in battle, a mighty man in the fight before his death-day, a champion in the charge in the van of armies; there fell five times fifty before his blades, of the men of Deira and Bernicia a hundred score fell and were destroyed in a single hour... Hyfeidd the Tall shall be honoured as long as there is a minstrel...

The men went to Catraeth, swift was their army, the pale mead was their feast, and it was their poison; three hundred men battling according to plan, and after the glad war-cry there was silence. Though they went to the churches to do penance, the inescapable meeting with death overtook them...

Red were their swords (may the blade never be cleansed), and white shields and square-pointed spear-heads before the retinue of Mynyddawg the Luxurious...

Artist's impression of an Anglo-Saxon woman and man from Norton in the Tees Valley. Most 6th century Northumbrian women adopted a western Scandinavian style of dress secured with brooches. The man's cloak was probably just a rectangle of coarser woollen cloth edged with braid. (Illustration: Terry Ball.)

The men went to Catraeth in column, raising the war-cry, a force with steeds and blue armour and shields, javelins aloft and keen lances, and bright mail-coats and swords. He led, he burst through the armies, and there fell five times fifty before his blades – Rhufawn the Tall, who gave gold to the altar and gifts and fine presents to the minstrel...

The warriors arose together, together they met, together they attacked, with single purpose; short were their lives, long the mourning left to kinsmen. Seven times as many English they slew; in fight they made women widows and many a mother with tears at her eyelids...

For the retinue of Mynyddawg I am bitterly sad, I have lost too many of my true kinsmen; of three hundred champions who set out for Catraeth, alas, but for one man none came back...

It is grief to me that after the toil of battle they suffered the agony of death in torment... after the battle, may their souls get welcome in the land of Heaven, the dwelling place of plenty.

Gododdin, by Aneirin. c. AD600 (I. Williams).

The northern British tribes, often divided and mutually hostile, were soon overrun by the Angles. But the Angles also fought one another. Aethelfrith was killed in battle in 616 when he fought a confederation of southern Angles led by Edwin the son of the heir to Deira. King Edwin was accepted as Aethelfrith's successor and became a 'Bretwalda', (a Bretwalda was, according to Bede, the 'over-king' of Britain) and further extended the power and influence of the kingdom of Northumbria. At its peak the kingdom embraced much of the land between the Humber and the Forth. By 633 Anglesey and the Isle of Man were brought under its influence and around 700 Rheged became a Northumbrian colony and Northumbrian Christian bishops exerted control over the whole of South West Scotland.

When King Edwin (616-633) was converted to Christianity in 627 (page 26) England was

Artist's impression of a Northumbrian king. The Northumbrian kings were warriors and would have worn a richer costume than other men, as well as helmets, mailcoats and swords. (Illustration: Terry Ball.)

on its way to becoming fully converted to the Roman Church. But Northumbria's expansionism was curbed by the pagan Anglo-Saxon King Penda of Mercia (a follower of Woden) when, in 632, he formed an alliance with the Christian British King of North Wales, Cadwallon. This fight between the Northern and Midland kingdoms was not a religious one – it was a power struggle for the control of Anglo-Saxon England. Penda and Cadwallon defeated and killed Edwin in 633 and Christianity faded in Northumbria.

Christianity, but this time that of the Celtic/Irish Church, was quickly revived in 635 by Edwin's successor King Oswald (Bretwalda and King, 634-642) when he invited Aidan, from the monastery of Iona, to Northumbria. Aidan created a monastery on Lindisfarne, a small island cut-off from the coast of Northumbria at high tide. The monastery was run on similar lines to the Ionan monastery.

The Welsh continued their alliance with Penda of Mercia and in 642 Oswald was killed at Oswestry. But in 655 Penda was himself beaten and killed by King Oswald's brother and successor Oswy (Bretwalda and King 642-670). Northumbria's southern expansionism was eventually brought to a halt when King Ecgfrith was defeated by the Mercians at the Trent in 679. The Northumbrians turned north but the Picts, having already suffered and lost much land (Argyle and Strathclyde) to the Northumbrians, fought back. They lured Oswy's son, King Ecgfrith, deep inside their own territory and, in 685, killed him in a battle which was fought on a site of their choosing. Northumbria's decline was sealed: Ecgfrith was the last of the Northumbrian Bretwaldas. Northumbria's decline was not only the result

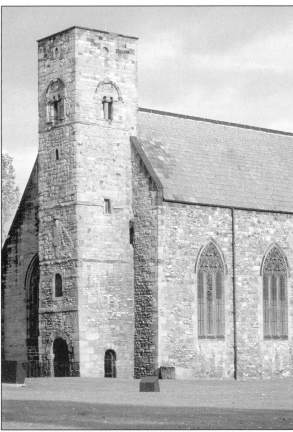

The western end of St Peter's Church, near the mouth of the River Wear, is today a tribute to the skill of Benedict Biscop's continental stone masons.

Artist's impression of the Anglo-Saxon monastery of St Paul at Jarrow, on the River Tyne, in the time of Bede. There were two churches and two main monastic buildings. The large riverside building was first used as a guest house and later as a workshop (Illustration: Ivan Lapper.)

of lost battles; corn from the rich, arable lands of the south could sustain more people, therefore there were more warriors there than in the north.

The Anglo-Saxon kings were passionate about religion and gave and willed away land and power to the Church with an almost excessive zeal. The Northumbrian kings especially diminished their power base by giving much to the Northumbrian Church. During the seventh century there was some rivalry between the Irish and Roman Churches. The main point of difference was on what day Easter should be celebrated, since the Irish Church used a different church calendar to the Roman Church. Ostensibly the Church rivalry was for the hearts and minds of the Anglo-Saxons, but in reality it was another power struggle – the submission of the English Celtic Church to the organisation and power of the Church of Rome. King Oswy made a dramatic and far-reaching decision in 664 at the meeting of the Synod of Whitby when he decided, partly due to the influence of his wife, in favour of the Roman Church. St Cuthbert, later Bishop of Lindisfarne monastery (685-687), accepted the dictate and passionately preached Roman Christianity in the remotest parts of Northumbria.

A young noblemen in King Oswy's court, Benedict Biscop, travelled to Rome with Wilfrid and then around Italy and Gaul visiting monasteries before returning to his native Northumbria. In 673 he persuaded Oswy's son, King Ecgfrith, to grant him land near the mouth of the River Wear where he built a church, St Peter's, and a monastery. Biscop used Gaulish craftsmen to build the stone church and Gaulish glaziers to produce England's earliest glass, forerunner of the famous glass industries of both Tyne and Wear. Biscop also built the monastery of St Paul at Jarrow on the Tyne in 681/682 – both monasteries following a variation of the disciplined rule of St Benedict and the Roman Church tradition. The library of St Peter's and St Paul's was probably one of the finest in the

Artist's impression of the basilica (large church) of St Paul as it may have looked in the eighth century. The church would have been bright and colourful, with painted panels and carvings. (Illustration: Ivan Lapper.)

country, even Europe, and much work was carried out copying manuscripts for missionary work in Britain and on the Continent. One of the finest manuscripts was the *Codex Amiatinus*, a magnificently illustrated Bible that was sent to Rome in 716. Without doubt the Venerable Bede wrote his *Ecclesiastical History of the English People* around 731 with the aid of the libraries.

Throughout the latter part of the seventh and for most of the eighth centuries the Northumbrian Church flourished and, as was to be expected, retained a powerful influence on secular as well as religious scholarship and learning. Today there are some outstanding relics of this period: Lindisfarne monastery produced the *Durham Echternach* and the world renowned *Lindisfarne Gospels*. The *Gospels* were copied and illustrated by Eadfrith, Bishop of Lindisfarne from 698 to 721, and the manuscript is an outstanding example of decorative art, one of the finest masterpieces of the insular (Anglo-Celtic) tradition and predates similarly-decorated, Irish manuscripts such as the *Book of Kells*. There are beautiful sculptured crosses, such as those found at Bewcastle and Ruthwell in South West Scotland (page 27); the wonderful Ormside bowl; and Caedmon's *Song of Creation*.

On the banks of the River Tyne at St Paul's monastery, the Venerable Bede (673-735) was England's first historian and his *Ecclesiastical History of the English People* (c. 731) probably the most important single source of early English history from 54BC to AD597 and of particular importance is the period 597 to 731, that was close to his own lifetime. Bede's scholarship could not have failed to influence the other great Anglo-Saxon churchman, the Northumbrian scholar and poet Alcuin (735-804), who left York's cathedral school at the invitation of Charlemagne to foster the revival of Latin literature throughout Charlemagne's Empire and to keep alive the Northumbrian tradition of art and learning. However this rich period of English learning and culture was soon to be devastated. The eighth and ninth century Viking invasions dislocated and destroyed Northumbrian Anglo-Saxon society and scholarship.

Mercia under King Penda had done much to destroy Northumbria's power, as did the West Saxons who pushed north into Northumbria under King Egbert of Wessex (page 27). By the end of the ninth century its power had further declined through internal strife and the kingdom was threatened on three fronts: Saxons from the South, Scots from the North and the Vikings from the East. It was the Norwegian Vikings who first plundered Lindisfarne in 793 and a year later attacked St Paul's monastery at Jarrow.

The Danish Vikings came to the Tyne in 875 under Halfdan, one of the leaders of the 'Great Army' (page 28) which in 874, after acting as a single force for nine years, was split into two. Tynemouth monastery was attacked and looted in 875 and for a year Halfdan's men skirmished with the Picts and the Britons of Strathclyde. He and his army settled round York c. 876.

Most of the large monasteries must have had scriptoria but the surviving manuscripts from Northumbria's 'Golden Age' are mainly from the Lindisfarne and Wearmouth-Jarrow monasteries. The illustration is a portrait of the Old Testament scribe from the Codex Amiatinus 1, f V, produced in the Wearmouth-Jarrow scriptorium sometime between 690-716.

The earliest example in European illumination of an illustration related to the text. It shows an initial H containing a portrait of Pope Gregory the Great and was completed in the Wearmouth-Jarrow scriptorium c. 747.

The monasteries on the Tyne and the Wear were again plundered in 914. This time it was by Norwegian Vikings, probably from Ireland, who were led by Ragnald. North East monasticism ground to a halt and was not revived for over 150 years (914-1075).

In 875, following the threat of another attack on Lindisfarne monastery, a few Lindisfarne monks carried St Cuthbert's body through wildest Northumbria and east into Cumbria. In 883, Guthred, the Danish King of York, finally allowed the monks, who called themselves the Community of St Cuthbert, to settle at Chester-le-Street. Bishop Eadred of the Community had supported Guthred's successful claim to the York throne and as a result in 884 the Danish king granted the Community large estates between the Tyne and Wear which had previously belonged to the monasteries of Jarrow and Wearmouth. The Community stayed at Chester-le-Street for

almost a hundred years until, in 995, they moved to another site on the River Wear at Durham, to start their rise to power which led to the advent of the mighty Norman Prince Bishops of Durham and the Durham Bishops were to become some of the most powerful men in Britain. A large twin-towered stone church, which became known as the 'White Church', was built to hold the remains of St Cuthbert.

Scotland, physically isolated by the Firth of Forth, was further cut off from the rest of England by the Norwegian Viking invasions and settlement of Ireland and Western Scotland and the Danelaw. It was thus the Vikings who, indirectly, were responsible for the creation of the new kingdom of Scotland which was formed when the Picts and Scots united in 844. Scotland became a formidable and long-standing threat to Northumbria. In 954 Eric Bloodaxe, the last Viking king of

Stone sculptures were introduced into Northumbria by Benedict Biscop and Wilfrid in the late seventh century. Skilled foreign masons produced carvings that were inspired by Mediterranean, Continental and insular styles. The fragment of a frieze from St Paul's, Jarrow shows a hunter in a plant-scroll and is from the early eighth century.

Northumbria, died and Northumbria ceased to be an independent kingdom. Its reduction to an earldom was reinforced in 960 when the Scots pushed down almost to the Tyne, destroying much of Northumbria.

Although the Danes had conquered most of Northern England, Danish settlement did not really extend much further north than the River Tees. Mercia and East Anglia became the Danelaw and no longer sovereign states. Bernicia, to the north of the Tyne, was still largely an Anglo-Saxon area and eventually became Northumberland. The remains of the once-mighty king of Northumbria's power still lay with the Anglo-Saxon earls of Northumbria, secure in the fortress of Bamburgh, once the stronghold of the Northumbrian royalty. From 921-954 the House of Bamburgh supported Anglo-Saxon Wessex against the Danish kings of York.

In the late tenth and early eleventh centuries the Viking invaders were more formidable and more successful in controlling the whole of

England than their ninth century ancestors. Canute's defeat of the Anglo-Saxon Edmund Ironside at Ashingdon in Essex in 1016 finally secured the northern Danelaw and Northumbria for the Danes. In 1017, with all England securely in his hands, King Canute divided his kingdom into the Earldoms of Northumbria, Mercia, East Anglia and Wessex.

Little is known of Pons Aelius, Corbridge (the other crossing point of the Tyne), and the monasteries of Jarrow and Wearmouth, during the second Viking invasions and the period before the Norman invasion. It is unlikely that the monasteries still existed although the associated churches could have continued to function. A pre-Norman name for Newcastle was 'Monkchester', an indication of a former Roman site that was possibly the site of a monastery. Perhaps a monastery was sited in or near the ruins of the Roman fort that once guarded Pons Aelius. The remains of a Christian cemetery, which dates from the eighth to the twelfth century, have been found

A beautiful (Urnes style) bronze mount from Tynemouth from the 10th-11th century AD.

to the west of Newcastle's Norman keep and this could have been the burial grounds of the monks of Monkchester or alternatively a graveyard for an Anglo-Saxon church that disappeared during the growth of the City of Newcastle. Monkchester lay on the old Roman route between Lindisfarne, Chester-le-Street and Durham and finds of coins suggest that it was developing as a small trading centre during the 800s. Corbridge, Jarrow and Wearmouth, where there have been eighth and ninth century coin finds, were also probably small centres of commercial activity.

The North East was the cultural centre and most powerful region in Anglo-Saxon England during the seventh and most of the eighth centuries. The region was then partly destroyed by the Scots, Saxons and Vikings. But tides turned and turned again. On the Wear the Norman Prince Bishops of Durham developed an almost sovereign state. Newcastle and Sunderland developed as two of the most important industrial and shipbuilding ports in the world and through 'King Coal' and the inventions and energies of the people and entrepreneurs who later lived and worked on the banks of the Tyne and the Wear the region played a dominant and important role in the Industrial Revolution and the evolution of Britain as the world's nineteenth century superpower.

Building New Castle.

CHAPTER FOUR

THE NORMAN CONQUEST: New and Dunholm Castles (c. 1000-1100)

King Edward the Confessor (King 1042-1066), elder son of Ethelred the Unready and Emma of Normandy, fled to Normandy at the time of Svein Forkbeard's invasions of England (page 30). He became king of England in 1042 but after more than 25 years in Normandy he was more Norman than English. He spoke French and appointed many Normans to positions of power. (It has been argued that the Norman Conquest of England started long before 1066!) Edward was a pious man and founded Westminster Abbey and had it designed by Norman architects. He married the daughter of Godwin, the powerful English Earl of Wessex, but their marriage was childless. Earl Godwin had placed Edward the Confessor on the throne and on Edward's death the throne passed to Harold II, Godwin's son and England's last Anglo-Saxon king.

The throne Harold inherited was not that of a powerful, united kingdom: the mighty earls of Northumbria and Mercia were unwilling to relinquish the power invested in them by King Canute. From across the North Sea and over the Channel, England looked ripe for invasion and in the autumn of 1066 two armies of invaders crossed the sea almost simultaneously: the Vikings from Norway, who believed they were Canute's rightful heirs, and the Normans from the Duchy of Normandy. In the north Harold Hardrada, the 'seven foot warrior' King of Norway, invaded Northumbria and occupied York. He was supported by Harold's brother Tostig who had once been the Earl of Northumbria. He was made Earl in 1055 by Edward the Confessor, but Tostig was a violent and frequently absent Earl and was supplanted by Morcar – with the approval of Edward and Harold. On Harold II's succession Tostig plotted to overthrow his brother and joined Harold Hardrada's invasion from Norway.

The Earls of Northumbria and Mercia attacked first, at the Battle of Fulford, and although badly beaten the Earls weakened the Norsemen. A few days later King Harold marched up from the south and attacked and destroyed the Vikings at Stamford Bridge. Tostig was killed during the battle and Northumbria was recovered.

Harold returned south to face the Normans led by William the Conqueror, the Duke of Normandy, but his battle-weary troops lost the Battle of Hastings when Norman cavalry cut down the Anglo-Saxon foot soldiers. The Earls of Northumbria and Mercia arrived too late to give Harold any assistance and he died – supposedly pierced through the eye by a Norman arrow. There was no upsurge of support by the people for a new English leader who could take the fight to William; gradually the southern part of England, already partly Normanised, capitulated. Bishops, earls and thegns swore allegiance to William who was crowned William I, King of the English, on Christmas Day 1066. In an extremely short space of time England received a new king, a new culture, a new language and a new aristocracy – the barons.

King William I (King of England 1066-1087) headed a powerful Norman baronage (that was Norse in origin), one of the most powerful military machines (mounted knights) and an efficient feudal power structure that under his leadership ruthlessly colonised Britain. Barons and knights controlled the serfs from almost impregnable castles that were first made of wood and later stone. The Barons controlled the knights who fought from the saddle as true cavalry, unlike the mounted infantry of the Anglo-Scandinavian thegns who dismounted and fought, less effectively, on foot. It is still remarkable that, even though Britain was not a united nation, William and perhaps some 10,000 Normans were able to control about 1.5 million people, many of whom were hostile, particularly those in the North.

By 1068 the South was subdued, but not the North. In the following year the Earls of Northumbria and Mercia, quiet at first, rebelled twice in 1069 and rebelled again in 1080. The Conqueror's revenge for the 1069 uprisings was cruel and swift. In the winter of 1069-1070 he took a violent revenge on both the land and the people of the North – the 'Harrying of the North' (see below). William obliterated Canute's four earldoms. The first to disappear was Wessex under Earl Godwin and, after their rebellions, Mercia and Northumbria. The Norman conquest of England was complete by 1070. In 1072 Malcolm III of Scotland submitted, although he continued to raid Northumbria until he was murdered.

William replaced English clergy with Normans, but resisted the authoritarian control of the Church of Rome. He cleverly separated the laws of the church from the laws of the state thereby laying the groundwork for the growth of English Common Law. Saxon 'shires' became Norman 'counties' and William, the king of all the land, governed through his Barons. The Domesday Book was created following the Domesday Survey of 1086 where each Manor's value and resources in the counties south of the River Tees and Ribble were recorded. The way was clear for the efficient collection of crown taxes, a successor of the Danegeld. William, although not introducing a continuous royal revenue, collected taxes first from the county and then the Lord of the Manor, the landowner. The landowner was responsible in turn for collecting/extracting the taxes from his tenants.

By the time William died in 1087, after a fall from his horse, the power in the church and the military was firmly in the hands of the Normans. The Norman Barons had land in England and Normandy and, in future, a well educated 'Englishman' or a member of the

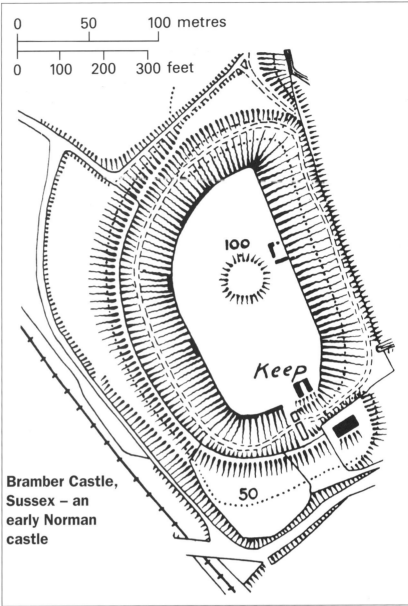

Bramber Castle, Sussex – an early Norman castle

In 1066 the Norman invasion fleet carried a 'prefabricated' wooden castle to protect their landing site at Hastings. Early Norman castles were earth mounds, mottes, with wooden palisades surrounding the top of the mound. The enclosure, the bailey, contained the buildings of a self sufficient community under the control of a Norman aristocrat who often lived in a 'great hall'. The later Norman castles were built of stone.
(From E.S. Armitage. Early Norman Castles of the British Isles, *1912)*

aristocracy would grow up to speak three languages – French, Latin and English. French and Latin were the favoured languages and for the aristocrats English looked set to disappear.

William was succeeded by his second son William II (King 1087-1100) or 'William Rufus', so named because of his red hair. He was shot while hunting in the New Forest. Henry I (King 1100-1135), the Conqueror's fourth and youngest son, succeeded. Henry I continued the fight to keep the power of the Roman Church at bay by following William's decision that the State, that is the king and not

Plate 1.
Artist's impression of the basilica (large church) of St Paul as it may have looked in the eighth century.
(Illustration: Ivan Lapper. Copyright: Bede's World, Jarrow.)

Plate 2.
Most of the large monasteries must have had scriptoria but the surviving manuscripts from Northumbria's 'Golden Age' are mainly from the Lindisfarne and Wearmouth-Jarrow monasteries. The illustration is a portrait of the Old Testament scribe from the Codex Amiatinus 1, f V, *produced in the Wearmouth-Jarrow scriptorium sometime between 690-716. (Copyright: Biblioteca Medicea-Laurenziana, Florence, Italy.)*

Plate 3.
Durham Cathedral's Sanctuary
Knocker. About 1140 and cast in
bronze. (Durham Cathedral Treasury.)

Plate 4.
The medieval Lindisfarne Priory, with Holy Island Castle in the background.

Plate 5.
A detail of St Cuthbert's coffin. The carving, made on English oak, is of the Virgin and Child. (Durham Cathedral Treasury.)

the Pope, should have the right to name the Bishops of England. Henry I spent much time on the continent defending the Duchy of Normandy; at one time fighting on three fronts against the Counts of Anjou and Flanders and the King of France, and consolidating the unity of his cross-Channel government of England and Normandy.

After centuries of internal strife between independent and rival kingdoms and a multitude of sea-borne invasions, Britain, under the Normans, gradually became a united country, stronger than the Anglo-Saxon kingdom of the English and strong enough to resist any further invasions. Viking expansionism finally ground to a halt as a united Anglo-Norman front, on the Continent and in England, blocked its movement westwards.

Two Rivers

The Normans did not bring a strong force to the North East of England until January 1069 when the newly appointed Norman Earl of Northumbria, Robert de Comines, arrived at Durham to avenge the death of Earl Copsig, William's first appointed Earl of Northumbria. Copsig had been killed at the village of Newburn on the north bank of the Tyne while trying to extort taxes from the Northumbrians. The local population attacked Durham at night and killed Robert de Comines along with 700 of his men. Flushed with success the Northumbrians marched on York, but William was able to relieve his garrison and suppress the first serious Northumbrian uprising.

A second uprising quickly followed when in the autumn of the same year a Danish fleet, led by the sons of the King of Denmark, landed in the Humber. Immediately it was supported by the Northumbrians and together they attacked and destroyed the Norman garrison at York. The rebellion spread to Mercia and Wales. William retaliated. He beat off the Danish invasion and during the winter of 1069/70 he burned the fields, towns and villages from York north to the River Tees. In County Durham the inhabitants fled across the River Tyne but their cattle were taken, many fields were scorched and houses destroyed.

In 1072 William returned to the north at the head of a large army and attacked the Scots who, under English speaking Malcolm III, had

never been conquered. Malcolm III (King of Scots, 1058-1093) became a vassal of William, although he continued to raid the north throughout the rest of his long reign. Malcolm died in a skirmish near Alnwick. On William's return south he was unable to cross the Tyne at Monkchester and he spent the night at the Tynemouth monastery.

Why William chose the site of Durham rather than Monkchester as the centre of his northern operations is unclear. Perhaps he considered Durham a better defensive site and it was well situated on the east coast lowland route to Scotland. The name 'hill island' or Dunholm was also applied to the surrounding region and in 1072 a second castle was built on the site of the old to guard the northern side of the meander loop which was most vulnerable to attack. In 1071, following the death of the last Saxon bishop, William appointed a Norman Bishop, Walcher of Lorraine.

In 1076 after the rebellion, capture and execution of Waltheof, the English Earl of Northumbria and youngest son of the pre-conquest Earl Siward of Northumbria, William the Conqueror combined the civil and military powers of the Earl of Northumbria with the Bishop of Durham which he conferred on Bishop Walcher.

In the early 1100s a strong stone wall was built round the periphery of the meander loop, replacing a wooden palisade. In 1093 work started on the magnificent Durham Cathedral to replace the Anglo-Saxon White Church. Progress was fast and by 1104 the Cathedral, constructed from locally quarried sandstone, was in use for services and the 'incorrupt' body of St Cuthbert laid in the new basilica. A new Benedictine priory was constructed next to the Cathedral and the land cleared between the castle and the Cathedral. Two bridges were built over to the meander loop, one at Framwellgate in 1128 and the other at Elvet in 1160 to link the peninsular to the surrounding land. The Benedictine Community grew in size and importance to the extent that some 200 years later there were over 100 members and among its dependent cells were Lindisfarne, Jarrow on the Tyne and Monkwearmouth on the Wear.

Set some distance south of the border, Durham castle and Bishop Walcher's Norman knights were unable to prevent the continued Scottish raids into Northumbria. The

The mound and octagonal shell keep of Durham Castle that was constructed in the year of Queen Victoria's accession. The first castle was built around 995 by the Community of St Cuthbert. It was attacked in 1006 and 1040 by the Scots. The Norman castle was built on the same site in 1072.

Northumbrians were further displeased by the arrogance and violence inflicted by the Norman knights on the local population. In 1080, guarded by 100 Norman knights, Walcher left Durham Castle to meet the protesting Northumbrian leaders at Gateshead. It was a rowdy meeting and at one point Walcher and his Norman retinue retired to a nearby church. The angry Northumbrians set fire to the church, killing Walcher as he tried to escape. The Northumbrians attacked the castle at Durham but after four days of unsuccessful siege they departed.

Once again William acted decisively, sending his half brother Odo, Bishop of Bayeux, to deal with the uprising. Working north from the Tees to the Tweed the Normans burned the manorial estates and killed many of the inhabitants. Many Anglo-Saxons fled to Scotland and this devastation caused by the Normans became known as the 'Harrying of the North'. William's revenge was recorded in the Domesday Survey (1086) which, although missing out the North East, described the condition of dozens of manors in the northern region as far north as Yorkshire as: 'it is waste'.

The experiment of combining the Earldom of Northumbria and the Bishopric of Durham was not continued and William appointed a Norman baron, with large holdings in the Midlands, as the new Earl of Northumbria. But the baron resigned and William's second choice for the Earl of Northumbria was Robert de Mowbray, who outlived the Conqueror.

However, the joint appointment of Walcher as Earl of Northumbria and Bishop of Durham, if only for four years, set an important precedent that subsequent Bishops of Durham were able to exploit and claim for centuries: the simultaneous holding of military, civil and ecclesiastical power. Durham Castle became the military and civil seat of the 'Palatine' while the Cathedral was the centre of the diocese. For years there were serious disputes between the Bishops and the Cathedral monastic community of which the Bishop of Durham was the titular abbot. The 'royal liberty of Durham' was to become one of the greatest feudal institutions in Medieval England and the heart of the 'Palatine' was the land between the Tyne and the Tees. Durham Cathedral, built by the second Norman Bishop of Durham, William de St Calais, was a symbol of the growing might of the Palatinate.

St Calais, a close adviser to William Rufus, was the first of the 'Prince Bishops' of Durham.

Many Northumbrians were forced to flee north during the 'harrying' while others, notably Gospatric, the heir to the Northumbrian earldom, chose to join English speaking Malcolm III rather than submit to the Normans. William still needed to defend the north against the Scots, who continued to raid Northumbria as far down as the River Tyne and who were in possession of the west coast of England as far south as Morecambe Bay. In 1080 William sent his eldest son, Robert Curthose, north to crush the Scots. Although the large army penetrated Scotland as far north as Falkirk, like the Romans he was unsuccessful in crushing Scotland and, like them, retreated to the River Tyne where he built the 'New Castle', a banked and ditched enclosure of wood and earth, on or near the site of the Roman fort at Monkchester. It was strategically well placed, between Durham Castle and Bamburgh Castle, and it is almost certain that the Roman bridge was rebuilt, or that a new bridge was constructed across the Tyne below the New Castle.

In a quick and efficient campaign in 1092 William Rufus had more success than his brother and secured Cumbria from the Scots. He built a castle at Carlisle with the result that the Tyne-Solway gap was secured. New Castle, with its bridge over the Tyne, quickly became an important military centre, a castle where armies could be gathered and supplied by sea and road and from which expeditions could be organised and dispatched.

Durham Cathedral dates back to 1093 and contains the remains of St Cuthbert and the Venerable Bede. Bede's remains were carried to the Cathedral in c. 1050 from the ruined Jarrow monastery. The medieval city of Durham was the administrative centre of the Prince Bishops.

New Castle was built in 1080 by Robert Curthose on a roughly triangular, defensible site. The site's south side rose up steeply from the Tyne and the north and east sides were protected by a ravine formed by the Lort Burn and a tributary. Robert Curthose had a deep ditch dug to protect New Castle's west side.
Newcastle Keep and Blackgate as they are today.

New Castle was attacked in 1095, when William the Conqueror's appointed Earl of Northumbria, Robert de Mowbray, rose up against William Rufus. Rufus sent an army north and recaptured the castle and from then on Newcastle remained a crown castle: the king, in order to maintain his own position of power, had to have a base from which to control his barons. Following the Earl's revolt the Northumbrian earldom was abolished and the king's administrative power was given to the lesser appointment: the Sheriff of Northumberland.

The Normans, by building New Castle on the River Tyne and Durham Cathedral and Castle on the River Wear, instigated the future cities of Newcastle and Durham. Durham Castle and Cathedral and New Castle were all part of the Normanisation of a subdued and conquered North, a region that was to remain under Norman feudal control for centuries. The feudal organisation and the Norman Castles were to play important roles in the forthcoming centuries of wars and Border disputes with Scotland. The Norman invasion broke forever the power of the Anglo-Scandinavian North and gave much of the

responsibility for its strategic defence to the Prince Bishops of Durham who, in return for their privileges, had to maintain a fortified garrison.

By the Middle Ages the Bishop of Durham was in an extremely powerful position; he levied taxes, raised troops, had his own mint, special forest jurisdiction (similar to the crown's) the right to all treasure trove on his extensive land and control over many of the region's rich coal and lead mines. The castle, priory and Bishop of Durham played a key role in the evolution of the settlements on the south bank of the Tyne and along the banks of the Wear. For centuries there were disputes between the developing and increasingly important town of Newcastle and the Bishop and priory of Durham.

The people of the North East, bowed but not beaten by the violence of William's 'Harrying of the North', managed to keep their spirit of independence alive. Their religious tolerance and rugged individualism, so much part of the Anglo-Scandinavian way, was not destroyed by the harsh Norman feudalism. Later these important characteristics were to serve them well.

CHAPTER FIVE

THE ANGLO NORMAN REALM: chivalry and stone castles (1100-1307)

Twelfth century England was now very much part of continental Europe, with the sea voyages across the Channel being undertaken relatively safely and easily – often quicker than the same distance by road. European and especially French culture dominated English architecture, music and art. French was the language of law, muse and courtier, while Latin was the language of learning and the writing of the (Anglo-Norman) Church. Records, charters, writs and documents proliferated and for the first time the serfs were forced to become involved with the written word, which was French or Latin. Anglo-Saxon, the tongue of Bede, was the spoken language of the serfs. It was some three centuries before Anglo-Saxon, simpler and much enhanced by French and Latin, became the rich, written prose and poetry of Chaucer, Shakespeare and Milton. The English language under the Anglo-Normans was, according to the historian G. M. Trevelyan, 'trodden under foot only to be trodden into shape'.

During the centuries of Anglo-Norman rule, despite attempts by the barons to reduce the power of the crown, the country was still governed by 'the king'. A king who was a poor manager of men always resulted in weak government. Thus any analysis of the period must centre around the kings. The Norman kings of England struggled to hold their possessions in England and the continent together – some were more successful than others. Stephen (1135-1154), grandson of William the Conqueror, plunged England into civil war.

Henry I was survived by his only legitimate daughter (he is said to have had over 20 bastards), Matilda. Despite marrying off eight of his illegitimate daughters to potential allies following the death of his only legitimate son, the politics of his succession dominated the end of his reign. Henry married off his daughter Matilda, after the death of her first husband, to Geoffrey Plantagenet, the son of the Count of Anjou, a province of west central France. This marriage eventually led to the creation of the 'Angevin Empire' which, at its height, stretched from the River Tweed to the Pyrenees.

On hearing of the death of his uncle Henry, Stephen hurried to England and, with the help of his brother, had himself crowned king. Mistakenly he allowed Henry's daughter Matilda, when she landed in southern England in 1138, to join her half brother Robert of Gloucester and make a claim on the throne: civil war was then inevitable. However the massive stone castles were almost impregnable and, although much energy was wasted and lands made waste, the war drifted on as a stale-mate and came to a temporary halt in 1148 when Matilda left England. Despite fighting on three fronts in order to preserve his continental possessions, Matilda's son Henry Plantagenet, the future King Henry II, landed in England in 1152 to make war on Stephen. A compromise was reached between Henry and Stephen when it was decided in 1153 by Treaty that on Stephen's death the crown was to pass to Henry Plantagenet – which it did in the following year.

During the civil war feudalism was at its peak, with barons and hundreds of castles controlling the land and the serfs. As a result of the compromise between Stephen and Henry, many castles were destroyed as power, after decades of civil strife, was reclaimed by the crown.

Henry II (1154-1189) married Eleanor of Aquitaine in 1152 and with marriage came land and great power, greater than that of the King of France. As soon as he came to the throne he set about reclaiming land lost to Scotland as a result of the weakening of the power of the crown during the civil war and regained Northumberland, Cumberland and Westmorland. He went on to conquer Ireland with the aid of 'Strongbow', the Earl of Pembroke, and on the continent he expanded the Duchy of Normandy and added the Duchy

A Medieval bronze water-ewer found in the South Tyne about four miles west of Hexham. The visor of the helm is closed and there are three bands of air-holes below the eye-slits. The body is covered in chain armour and the lack of elbow or knee-pieces dates the mounted warrior to the beginning of the thirteenth century, as does the pattern on the saddle straps and the surcoat border.

of Brittany to his Duchy of Aquitaine and Countship of Anjou. Although Henry II spent only a third of his 34 year reign in England, he reduced the power of the Anglo-Norman barons partly by overhauling the judicial system and centralising it around royal courts rather than the local magnates. 'Common Law', the originally unwritten part of English law which is based on 'common customs', was developed onwards from the Norman Conquest and was based on 'judicial precedent' – that earlier judgments had to apply to similar cases. Henry II ruled that Common Law was to originate from a single royal source, which was to replace the hotchpotch of local communal jurisdictions and courts that were the legacy of Anglo-Scandinavian England. Trial by jury rather than trial by ordeal or battle was introduced in his reign. Jurymen were expected to offer their own local knowledge and experience as part of the proceedings. He was a great and powerful king but although Henry II's two surviving sons, Richard and John, both became kings, by the end of King John's reign the mighty Angevin Empire was no more.

By forming an alliance with the King of France, Richard I (1189-1199), nicknamed Coeur de Lion, secured his inheritance as the head of the Angevin Empire. His father Henry II had made him Duke of Aquitaine in 1172 and Richard spent most of his life and reign either on the continent or on crusade – spending only five months in England. In 1190 he set out with the King of France on the Third Crusade and took Messina, Cyprus and Acre. Although failing to recapture Jerusalem, he negotiated a settlement with his able opponent Saladin that allowed the crusader states to survive for another 100 years. England was governed in his absence by well chosen ministers who effectively looked after Richard's interests and the affairs of the crown. Returning from the crusade Richard I was imprisoned in Austria for over a year and only released on payment of a huge ransom. At the time of his capture the Angevin Empire was still intact but while in prison he lost part of it, notably Normandy, to the King of France. On his release he recovered most of his possessions but died heirless on the continent in a minor skirmish.

His brother John (1199-1216), nicknamed Lack-land or Soft-sword, started badly by losing Richard's gains to the King of France, retaining only a small part of Aquitaine (1204-1205). With his continental campaign in disarray, John returned to England and, unlike most of the Plantagenets, he remained there for much of his reign. He raised taxes in attempts to continue the war with the King of France and fell out with Rome over the appointment of the Archbishop of Canterbury – the Pope excommunicated him and ordered all English churches to close for six years. John retaliated by confiscating the estates of the Church but the churches remained shut. He conceded to the Pope's demands in 1213 but at the cost of becoming the Pope's vassal.

John's failure to recover his lost continental lands and his increasing unpopularity brought him into conflict with his barons. The barons rebelled and in 1215, after they had captured London, John was forced to sign the Magna Carta which removed some of his powers and is the basis of the English constitution. The Pope condemned and cancelled Magna Carta and John's almost immediate rejection of the Charter led to the first Baron's War (1215-1217). The defiant barons formed an alliance with Louis, the son of the King of France, and invited him to England. But the baronial and French army was defeated at Lincoln in 1217 after John's death.

John's death in 1216, traditionally from a 'surfeit of peaches and cider', marks the end of the cross-Channel Norman legacy. As the continental territories were gradually lost, English unity began to grow and the disaffected barons, although continuing to speak French, were increasingly concerned with their English estates and eventually the growth of England. John's son Henry III (King 1216-1272) was a minor and the 'Minority Council' was formed to govern until he came of age. The Council won victories over the barons at sea and on land and Louis was forced to return to the continent but the Minority Council, under the control of Hubert de Burgh, was able to placate the barons by amending Magna Carta to further weaken the power of the crown. (Magna Carta was reissued three times after 1215: 1216, 1217 and 1225.) Henry III became king in 1216, but by then little remained of the Plantagenet's French possessions: the Minority Council had been less concerned with the continental part of the Angevin Empire than with their immediate problems in England.

Henry III, happily married to a French wife,

surrounded himself with unpopular French advisers and, trying to raise large amounts of money to conquer Sicily for his son, the barons objected. They attempted to remove government from the hands of the king with the Provisions of Oxford and Westminster but civil war followed when Henry renounced the Provisions. His son Edward defeated the barons at the battle of Evesham in 1265. The barons' defeat brought about a compromise and, in the latter part of his reign, much of the power of the monarchy was restored although part of the Provisions of Westminster and the reissues of the Magna Carta were accepted by Henry.

Henry's son Edward I ('Longshanks', King 1272-1307) was on his way back from a crusade when he heard of his father's death. On his return to England in 1274, after residing in Gascony, the remaining continental Plantagenet possession, he became much involved in English affairs. He immediately set up an investigation into the corrupt activities of the officials of both the barons and the crown which was to result in widespread legislation. He set up a consultative body with regard to the raising of taxes which was known as the 'parliament'; it was the fore runner of modern parliament. He used the Anglo-Norman barons to subdue Wales for the crown and, to consolidate his position, built a series of immensely strong Welsh castles. Edward installed his son as the first English Prince of Wales in 1301 and, stubbornly intent on asserting his authority over all the British Isles, turned his attention to Scotland.

Since the eleventh century most of Scotland had been ruled by one king, the King of the Scots. The Scot Kenneth MacAlpine had over-run the Picts (in 844) to create a kingdom centred round Scone on the River Tay. For generations Celtic Scotland had clashed with Lothian, the rich lowlands north east of the River Tweed that were once part of the Anglo-Saxon kingdom of Northumbria, before the kingdom disintegrated under the Viking invasions (Chapter 3). At one time South West Scotland had also been part of Northumbria (page 32) but the border moved south, crossing the Tyne-Solway gap to the Lake District as the Scottish nation became more structured and the power of the kingdom of Northumbria waned.

In time the Scottish capital moved from Scone to the fortress at Edinburgh and the Scottish Kings became English speaking. From the period when Scotland was ruled by Malcolm III (King 1058-1093) the people of Galloway and Strathclyde slowly adopted the English language and feudal ways. King Malcolm had spent his childhood in the court of Edward the Confessor and with the help of his uncle Siward, Earl of Northumbria, reclaimed the Scottish crown, killing Macbeth, who in 1057 had usurped his throne by killing his father King Duncan in battle. Scotland was further reinforced by refuge-seeking Northumbrians as they fled north away from the Norman knights during the 'Harrying of the North'.

Scotland was too remote and the terrain too difficult for the southern-based, Anglo-Norman kings to consider its total conquest although Malcolm III, for example, was forced to pay tribute to William the Conqueror. The result was that the richer and more powerful English-speaking kings of lowland Scotland expanded north and attempted to include the Scottish Highlanders in their kingdoms. They were not entirely successful and Scottish Celtic ways survived in the remote Highlands more or less intact until the eighteenth century.

King David I (King 1124-1153, the youngest son of Malcolm III) was educated at the court of Henry I of England. He was well aware of the effectiveness of the Norman military machine, especially the mounted knight, and he invited Anglo-Norman warriors (like the Bruces) into his kingdom and gave them baronies. David used traditional Norman methods – conquering, castle-building and a rigid feudal system – to expand his realm northwards and westwards. He supported the claims of his niece Matilda (page 47) to the English crown and advanced his army over the border into England in 1137 in support of her civil war against Stephen. The Anglo-Scottish border had remained fluid from Roman times but in the reign of William II it settled along the Tweed-Solway line where it remains today. When David crossed the border into England in support of Empress Matilda it was the start of the 'Auld Alliance' between Scotland and France, which often resulted in Scotland attacking England after encouragement from France. In 1137 David advanced to the Tees and, by-passing Durham castle where Bishop Geoffrey Rufus remained loyal to Stephen, he headed south only to be met near Northallerton by a combined force of the

Bamburgh Castle was a Northumbrian king's castle. The king supported Anglo-Saxon Wessex against the Vikings. The Vikings destroyed much of the castle. The Normans rebuilt; it decayed and was massively reconstructed by the Victorian, Tyneside industrialist, Lord Armstrong.

Archbishop of York and the mail-clad, Anglo-Norman Yorkshire barons, both ably supported by a new potent weapon – the English yeoman archer. David was well beaten at the Battle of Standard in 1138, but King Stephen, unable to follow up England's advantage, made a truce and ceded Northumberland to David I in 1139, the Scottish king's son becoming the Earl of Northumberland. King David held Northumberland from 1139 to 1157, as well as overrunning Cumbria and parts of Lancashire.

As part of the truce Bamburgh castle and the royal castle of Newcastle were to remain in the hands of the English crown, but there are records of King David holding his court in Newcastle and, thus ensconced, David might well have built St Andrew's church. By the time he died in 1153 he had founded over a dozen monasteries. He was succeeded by his son, but

the powerful English King Henry II met him at Chester in 1157 and, without an arrow being fired, persuaded the Scots to return to the Tweed Solway line and relinquish Northumberland, along with Cumbria and Westmorland, to the English crown.

William I ('The Lion', King 1165-1214), grandson of David I, crossed the border again in 1174, this time with a huge army. He could not take Prudhoe Castle but besieged Alnwick. The Sheriff of Yorkshire, lost in fog at the head of an advance party of 400 mounted men from the main English army, found himself in the middle of William's camp when the mists cleared! In a superb piece of opportunism he captured William and after being held briefly at New Castle William was taken to Rouen. Under the Treaty of Falaise, William I was ransomed for money and five of Scotland's most powerful castles, one of which was the massive Edinburgh castle. He became a vassal of the English throne but on Henry II's death in 1189 William purchased Scotland's independence from Henry's son, Richard I. Scotland abandoned its attempts to annex Northumberland and in 1237 at the Treaty of York it formally gave up its claim to northern English soil.

Although Scotland and England had had peaceful relations through much of the thirteenth century, Edward I started a long and bitter feud with Scotland. His son, later Edward II, was betrothed to marry the heir to the Scottish throne, thereby peacefully attaching Scotland to England, but when she died, at the age of six, Edward I demanded the right to decide who should be their next king of Scotland. He chose John Balliol, who was crowned king in 1292.

Edward I's determination to master Scotland was to lead to almost three centuries of protracted and unprofitable war. Edward chose John Balliol, a baron who had large Scottish and English estates, over another powerful Scottish baron Robert Bruce, but politically weak Balliol found it difficult to appease both Edward and the Scottish nobility. On 26th December 1292 he swore fealty to the English crown at Newcastle. An uneasy peace existed until 1296 when English ships were burnt in Berwick upon Tweed. Edward I, 'the hammer of the Scots', invaded Scotland, removed the Scottish coronation stone from Scone to Westminster and declared himself King of Scotland. But Edward I, despite defeating the Scots and like many others before him, was unable to crush them.

In 1297 William Wallace, an unknown knight and largely unsupported by the Scottish Anglo-Norman barons, defeated an English army at Stirling and set himself up as the 'Guardian' of Scotland. He invaded and took the English castle at York. Edward I hurried

Prudhoe Castle c. 1880. Robert Umfraville was the first of a long line of Norman barons who were Lords of Prudhoe castle for some 300 years. The castle was erected during the reigns of Stephen and Henry II and it was Odinel de Umfraville who held the castle against the Scottish attack led by William the Lion.

north and defeated Wallace at Falkirk in 1298 by the deadly combination of mounted knights and English and Welsh longbowmen. But William Wallace escaped and continued to lead an effective and popular campaign against the English before he was captured in 1305 and taken to London to be hung, drawn and quartered. Robert Bruce, who had sworn fealty to Edward I in 1296 as Earl of Carrick, changed sides and joined Wallace's rebellion. Bruce stabbed his political rival to death to become the Scottish King and he went on to defeat the English at Loudoun Hill in 1307. Edward I died in 1307 on his way to fight Bruce.

Scotland was to become a dangerous foe for the emerging English nation. In the three centuries of border wars that followed the strategically and increasingly important towns and castles of Newcastle and Durham played vitally important roles.

The Newcastle keep was built by Henry II. The walls of the square keep are reinforced with flat, pilaster buttresses; there is a thickened base, or plinth, and strong corner turrets. The outward projecting battlements are an incorrect, nineteenth century restoration. The second floor entrance to the keep is unusually high and is covered by two turrets. A towered, stone, curtain wall with north and south gateways was built round the Norman bank.

Two Rivers

King Henry II spent much of his life travelling throughout his extensive realm which stretched from the Tweed to the Pyrenees, meeting local magnates, distributing justice and, amongst much else, rebuilding and inspecting his castles, the symbol and the power of the Norman feudal overlord. Between 1167-1178 he rebuilt New Castle in stone at a cost of £1,444. The original New Castle was constructed by Robert Curthose of earth and wood on a natural, defensive site. This was a triangular ridge protected on two sides by deep ravines cut by the Lort Burn and its tributary and a steep cliff that formed the base of the triangle which led to the banks of the River Tyne. The west side of the original castle was further protected by a deep, man-made ditch from which clay was used to level the site and build high banks. The stone outer walls of Henry II's castle were built on the existing earthen banks and surrounded a massive rectangular stone tower that was the work of Maurice 'the engineer'. There were circular towers in the walls and a north and west gate. In 1173 when William I of Scotland attacked the castle, it stood firm although only partially completed. King John added a large single storey building to the east wall of the castle, with a main hall measuring some 66ft by 44ft (24m by 16m) with extensive kitchens to the north and royal chambers to the south. The Black Gate (page 46), a fine example of mid-thirteenth century military engineering and the main outer gateway to the castle, was added to the stone wall between 1247 and 1250. The 'Half Moon' could have been added to strengthen the south-eastern section and to oversee the bridge below.

From the onset of the building of the stone castle, traders and merchants had gathered round the walls for protection: the town and later city of Newcastle were beginning to grow. Around 1200 stone-faced, clay-filled finger jetties were built in the river and the Tyne began to play an increasingly important role in Newcastle's growth in a period when the Roman roads sank into disrepair and sea transport became the most important means of

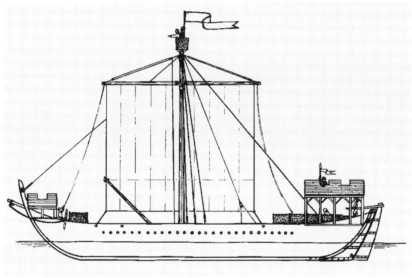

The Tyne Galley.

communication. Recent archaeological excavations at Newcastle's quayside show that the town invested large amounts of money developing the waterfront so as to increase the ability of the town to handle shipping and merchandise. The present day quayside is some 300ft away from the bank that rises up to the city. It was perhaps as early as 1100 when the hillside was terraced and the river pushed away from the bank. During the 1200s the river bank was built up behind a retaining wall and the stone-faced finger jetties reached out into the river from individual properties. The areas between the jetties were gradually filled with rubbish and in the late fourteenth century a

continuous waterfront was built. In 1275 Newcastle was the sixth largest wool port in England. Principal exports from medieval Newcastle were wool, timber and coal, as well as mill stones, dairy produce, fish, salt and hides.

From the middle of the thirteenth century the Hanseatic League played a major role in the development of trade around the North Sea. The League, developed when a number of German trading towns banded together to defeat piracy and form a trading alliance, was responsible for the development of the family of cargo ships that were known as Hanseatic cogs. These were impressive ships for their time, clinker built with a single mast and square sail and, from about 1250, had the latest development in ship technology – a stern hung rudder. They sailed as far south as the Mediterranean and one of the first recorded movements of ships in the River Tyne is in 1294 when a group of 11 cogs arrived at the quayside 'driven into our port by tempest' and on behalf of Edward I their cargoes were seized and the ships sold. Newcastle was already developing as an important port, its merchants trading with the Baltic and North sea coasts of Germany. By the end of the thirteenth century Newcastle was a port of second rank behind London and it was not surprising that King Edward chose it to build a war galley as part of a 20 ship order to the country's most important sea ports. It was built at the mouth of the Lort Burn and completed in 1295. A detailed financial inventory was made of the galley but there are no records of its appearance or size. One estimate, made from the inventory, makes the galley 130ft (39.6m) long, with an 18ft (5.5m) beam and perhaps 30 oars on each side, a stern-hung rudder and a single mast and square sail. The Newcastle galley was used against the Scots for a couple of years before being sold back to Newcastle in 1301 for £40.

Newcastle's earliest classification, possibly made during the reign of Henry I, was as a borough, a fortified town with special rights,

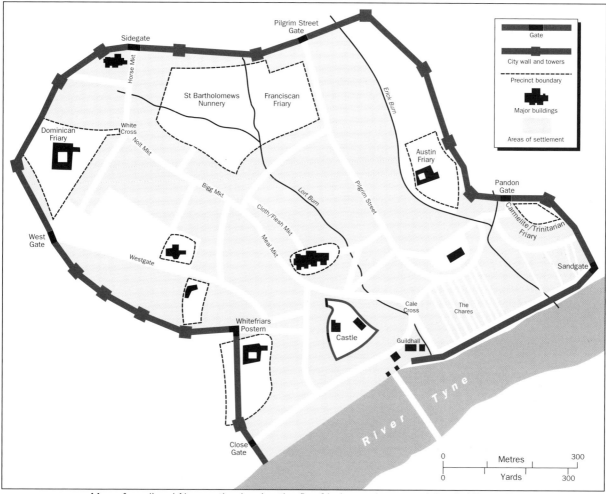

Map of medieval Newcastle showing the five friaries and nunnery (after R J Buswell).

which made it distinct from a manorial village or small town. In feudal times Newcastle was under the control of the king whose power was exerted through the Sheriff, a local Norman baron. The Sheriff was ultimately responsible for the town courts, markets and the 'firma burgi' – the collection of rents, fines, tolls etc which he paid to the King. As Newcastle grew its townspeople wanted more control over their own lives and they obtained this by a series of charters that extended over 500 years. Its earliest known charter is dated 1175 in the reign of Henry II when the town's burgesses were exempted, amongst other things, from paying a toll for the use of the Tyne. The firma burgi was eventually fixed and paid by the town directly to the Exchequer and, amongst other 'liberties', Newcastle gained control of its courts and was able to appoint its own bailiffs. The firma burgi became known as the 'fee farm' because the crown's taxes were 'farmed' out to be collected by those other than the King's officers. Creating a fixed farm fee was advantageous to the town as it made Newcastle

more independent of the crown and in inflationary times the burgesses knew their level of expenditure. In 1201 John raised the fee farm from £50 to £60 per annum. More importantly, just before his death in 1216, King John increased Newcastle's independence by granting the town a mayor. In the same year he allowed the formation of guilds which were known as the 'Mysteries' from *corps de metier* (French for 'guild'). Merchant guilds formed cartels and restricted trade so that visiting merchants were only allowed to buy through the burgesses of the town. Initially there were twelve guilds which were not only good for local trade, by creating cartels, they were also mutually supportive bodies that attended to the spiritual and material needs of their members. By 1300 Newcastle was governed by a Mayor and four Bailiffs who were associated with the 'Council of Twenty Five' which were elected by the leading guilds.

'Sea coal' was being exported from 1250 and by 1281 some significant shipments were being made. By 1350 the burgesses had received a royal licence to export coal and soon coal was to replace wool as the town's main export. By the end of the fourteenth century coal exports to Holland, France and Flanders were booming – Newcastle was on its way eventually to become the coal capital of the world.

The burgesses continued to consolidate their town and further its independence. Ever aware of the town's vulnerability to the Scottish invaders they decided to enclose it within a massive wall. The money was raised by a special 'wall tax' – the *murage*, from the Latin mur for wall – and building started shortly after 1265 when the tax was allowed. It probably took about 100 years to complete the wall and although the aim was to include the castle as a citadel within the wall, this was abandoned so that the western quayside could be included within the wall, along with many of the more powerful burgesses' homes! A large ditch, the King's Dyke, was dug outside the walls and completed before 1317. The Dyke was some 35ft (10.5m) wide and 12ft (3.6m) deep and dug close to the walls, which when completed were a formidable defence – two miles long (3.3km), around 9ft (2.7m) thick, some 25ft (7.5m) high and containing 17 towers all within bowshot of each other. There were six main gates and at least four smaller gates and posterns. One result of enclosing the town with such a powerfully defensive wall was that the defensive role of the castle became less important and from around 1300 the castle began a slow decline.

The town expanded rapidly in the thirteenth century, growing mainly on the land north of the castle; most of the early development was to the west of the Lort Burn. Although medieval Newcastle had no great cathedral within the town walls it did have five friaries and the friars were much involved with the daily life of the townspeople. The Blackfriars or Dominicans was an order that was founded in 1216 by St Dominic and the friars had arrived in Newcastle by 1239. It was an important friary in that it became the residence of visiting monarchy – for example Edward II and Queen Isabella stayed there. The town walls were even breached by a small narrow gate to allow the friars access to their garden which was divided in two by the walls. Other friaries within the walls belonged to the Whitefriars or Carmelites, who settled there in 1262; the Austinfriars, 1290; the Greyfriars or Franciscans, 1274; and the Trinitarians. The oldest religious house was St Bartholomews, the nunnery, perhaps founded as early as 1086 and situated near present day Nun Street, and a home for the religious daughters of the gentry (Map, page 55).

The burgesses fought hard to keep their trading monopolies and control over trade and navigation on the Tyne. In the 1300s, for example, they tried to prevent ships from mooring on the south side of the river and fish from being landed at South Shields. In 1352 the mayor even went as far as to seize South Shields' fishing boats, forcing the owners to swear that they would only sell fish in the Newcastle market. Inevitably they clashed with the ever-expanding powers of the Durham Bishops and Cathedral.

The Bishop of Durham was a powerful feudal magnate, eventually owning nearly all of the land between the Tyne and the Tees, much of the land given to the Community of St Cuthbert by the devout Anglo-Saxon

Durham Cathedral: "Half house of God, Half castle 'gainst the Scots" (Sir Walter Scott).

The remains of the medieval Lindisfarne priory. The priory was built in 1093 over St Aidan's monastery, but became a ruin in the sixteenth century.

Christian kings. Since the Norman conquest the church and lands had been detached from the earldom of Northumbria and given to the bishop who also had titular control over Durham Cathedral, Castle and Priory although the estates of the Priory were distinct from those of the Bishop. Hugh Le Puiset, King Stephen's nephew, became Bishop of Durham in 1153 and added much to the power and wealth of Durham. Around 1150 the Benedictine Community under the Prior of Durham was expanded to include the refounded Jarrow, Wearmouth and Lindisfarne monasteries. Bishop Hugh Le Puiset provided a large contingent for King Richard's crusade and he acted as a regent to raise money for the crown in Richard's absence. The Bishop purchased large tracts of land north of the Tees, Barnard and Hartlepool castles and during his lifetime was the Earl of Northumberland. In 1180 he created the so-called 'Boldon Book' to catalogue the bishop's enormous estates in Durham and Northumberland along lines similar to the Domesday Book (page 42) which had excluded Northumberland and Durham when it was compiled. Interestingly there are references to

'coalsmiths' at Bishopwearmouth and 'colliers' at Escomb, forerunners of the thousands of coal miners who were later to work the region.

The estates of the Cathedral Priory were not included in the Boldon Book as the Priory and its monks were becoming an increasingly separate body. By the Middle Ages the Bishop of Durham was extremely powerful. As the major landowners between the Tyne and the Wear the Bishop and the Priory played key roles in developing the settlements along both banks of the Wear and the south banks of the Tyne. For centuries there were disputes between Newcastle and the Bishop of Durham who claimed one half of the River Tyne and marked the northern limit of his lands by the 'Cuthbert Stones', blue stones that were set in to the footway of the medieval Tyne bridge. Newcastle claimed to own two thirds of the Tyne bridge and there were constant arguments over the control of navigation rights on the river, the Newcastle bridge and the export of coal from the mines at Gateshead and Whickham. The disputes declined as the kings of England broke the power of the Prince Bishops of Durham.

CHAPTER SIX

WAR AND MORE WAR: burgess and bishop
(1300-1500)

The fourteenth and fifteenth centuries were turbulent times as England waged war notably against Scotland and France, as well as Ireland, the Low Countries and Wales. When not fighting, most people worked the land. Sheep rearing and wool production continued to be a major industry and wool was still being exported to the Flemish Lowlands despite a growing English cloth-manufacturing industry. Fishing, salt-making and mining were other important occupations.

The condition of the peasantry varied markedly during the two centuries. The population reached a peak of around four million by the end of the thirteenth century with the result that there was insufficient arable land. The landowners had a large pool of cheap labour which drove down wages. There was a series of bad harvests in the early 1300s which was followed by the Black Death, recurring bubonic plague spread by rats, in 1348 and again in the 1350s and 70s. The result was a reduction in the population by about a third, and a labour shortage. Although they paid a terrible price, the peasants who survived were able to improve their working conditions and end the system of labour rents and serfdom. The constant wars with France meant constant taxes, including the poll tax, which caused more poverty. The peasantry rose up in 1381 in the 'Peasants' Revolt'.

English kings were murdered or deposed and dynastic wars rocked the English nation. As in the previous two centuries the king, the royal family and the barons were the centre of government, the king remaining the focal point. The main concern of government throughout the two centuries was political instability and making war. The crown passed to the king's eldest son. Weak kings generally resulted in weak governments and lost possessions; strong kings conquered and gained control of government and lands. Although there were irregular assemblies of Parliament, at most once a year, it gradually increased its power and its role in government – usually strengthening its position during the reign of weak kings. Parliament developed a monopoly on tax raising – the king needed to have some system for obtaining his subjects' consent for his ever increasing need for money to wage war.

Edward I 'Longshanks' was a strong king but his son Edward II (King 1307-1327) was weak, easily influenced and unstable. Edward II was no match for the Scots who, led by Robert Bruce (page 53) and the Douglas family, regained castles and land from the Anglo-Normans. Edward II was insecure and strongly influenced by his favourites, especially the Gascon, Piers Gaveston, who was later

Robert the Bruce's stone in Galloway Forest which marked the beginning of his successful campaign against the English.

The 1346 battle of Neville's Cross fought outside Durham which resulted in the defeat of David II of Scotland. The painting is from Froissart's Chronicle and depicts the violent nature of many medieval conflicts. The romanticised walled town is neither Durham nor Newcastle.

murdered by the barons in 1312. Edward's unpopularity with the barons increased with his disastrous Scottish campaign against Robert Bruce. Robert Bruce became Robert I, King of Scotland (1306-1329), and soundly defeated Edward II in 1314 at Bannockburn – a mobile Scottish army destroying much of the chivalry of England. Edward II lost control of his kingdom to a group of magnates, the Lords Ordainers, led by the Earl of Lancaster. Although Edward managed to regain control of his kingdom and execute Lancaster he was once again influenced by a favourite, much to the displeasure of his powerful magnates. In 1327 they forced him to assent to his own abdication in favour of his fifteen year old son Edward III. Edward II was then murdered at Berkeley Castle by the instigation of his own wife Isabella of France and her lover Roger Mortimer.

Edward III (King 1327-1377) was a powerful and chivalrous king although a poor administrator. He soon asserted his power by having his father's murderer Roger Mortimer hanged and continued the Scottish wars winning a major victory at Halidon Hill in 1333. Even though he was able to place John Balliol's son, Edward, on the Scottish throne the Scottish wars ground on. They lasted,

mainly as guerrilla warfare, for some 250 more years along the Borders, arguably more harmful to Scotland as England's economic power and trade developed.

Edward III went to war with France, claiming the French crown through his mother Isabella. In 1337 he embarked on the first of a series of campaigns that were to become known as the Hundred Years War. He had great success at first with victory at sea (Sluys, 1340) and on land at Crecy (1346) and Poitiers (1356) where the yeomen's longbow cut down the armoured knights of France. Throughout his campaigns he was ably aided by his son Edward, the Black Prince (1330-1376), and together they regained the Duchy of Aquitaine. Gascony was still in English hands and continued a healthy trade, with French wine being exchanged for English corn and cloth. The Black Prince ruled his father's possessions of Aquitaine and Gascony but, like his father, he was a better warrior than administrator. He died before his father. During Edward III's reign Parliament continued to raise taxes for the king's successful war efforts.

King David II of Scotland (King 1329-1371), the son of Robert Bruce, was forced into exile in France by Edward Balliol, but taking advantage of Edward III's absence in France returned to Scotland in 1341. David II invaded England but was defeated by the combined forces of Lord Percy and Bishop Neville at Neville's Cross in 1346. He was imprisoned and ransomed for a huge sum of money which was only half paid when he died in 1371.

A senile King Edward III died in 1377 and was succeeded by Richard II (1377-1399), the ten year old son of Edward, the Black Prince. A minority council ruled England on his behalf and the council's introduction of a poll tax to raise money for war with France and the lack of success in the French wars, coupled with the horror of the Black Death, led to the Peasant's Revolt in 1381. Richard had some success in dealing with the revolt and tried to take control of his kingdom but was frustrated by the council. He raised an army, reconquered Ireland (which had increasingly drifted away from English Anglo-Norman control) and exerted his authority, wisely at first but increasingly despotically as he arbitrarily executed or murdered those he perceived to be his enemies. Although the English were defeated at a number of skirmishes by the Scots, notably Otterburn in 1388, the Scots never had the power or resources to conquer England. Richard II continued Edward I's war of attrition against the Scots with a number of military campaigns and the well tried English policy of supporting dissident Scottish magnates.

Richard quarrelled with, and exiled, his cousin Henry Bolingbroke and made the mistake of sequestering the Lancastrian lands of John of Gaunt, Henry Bolingbroke's father, when he died in 1399. Henry Bolingbroke's timely return to England while Richard was away in Ireland enabled him to claim the crown as Henry IV. The powerful Percy and Neville families, earls of Northumberland and Westmorland, supported Bolingbroke, playing a crucial 'kingmaker' role in what was essentially a *coup d'état*. On his return from Ireland Richard surrendered and was imprisoned in Pontefract Castle where he died mysteriously.

Henry IV's reign (King 1399-1413) was not an easy one. He fought and overcame the Scottish under Douglas, the Welsh and the mighty Percy family. The Percys shifted their allegiance but Henry IV defeated Hotspur, the Earl of Northumberland's son, at Shrewsbury in 1403 when Hotspur was on his way to link forces with the Welsh. The Scots, ever keen to

seize an opportunity, linked up with the Percys but they were defeated at Bramham Moor in 1408, when the Earl of Northumberland was killed. For much of his reign Henry IV lived and fought from the saddle and, although a strong king, was forced to bend to some of Parliament's demands. He did however strengthen the power of the crown following the weak reigns of Edward II and Richard II and, producing four legitimate sons, there were no dynastic problems of succession.

His son Henry V (King 1413-1422) reinstated the disgraced Percys and united the English nation by renewing Edward I's claim on the crown of France. Under Henry V at Agincourt in 1415 the English and Welsh longbowmen, vastly outnumbered, destroyed the flower of French chivalry. Henry V was a strong and powerful king unlike his son Henry VI (King, 1422-1462 and 1470-1471) who, as a result of the fierce military campaigns of his father, was the only English king to be crowned both king of France and England. During Henry V's reign the constant warfare with France resulted in the English developing a hatred of all things French. He discouraged the use of the French language and English, so long 'trodden under' and the language of the serfs, reemerged and was slowly reinstated as the language of government, court and literature.

Gentle King Henry VI was an unpopular, weak and unsuitable ruler and lost first Normandy and then Gascony in 1453 to the French. The claims to the throne by Richard, Duke of York, led to the dynastic Wars of the Roses. Edward IV (King 1461-1483), son of Richard, Duke of York, eventually gained the throne and proved himself a capable ruler by much improving the English economy by encouraging trade with the Continent.

Edward V was only twelve when his father Edward IV died. Edward V was one of the princes who were murdered in the Tower of London possibly by their uncle Richard III. Richard III (King 1483-1485) was killed at Bosworth in 1485 by Henry Tudor, after landing from France at Milford Haven. By then England was war-weary and Henry VII (King 1485-1509), whose hereditary claim was tenuous, managed to hang on to the crown and end the Wars of the Roses. He built a strong administration and replenished the king's treasury ready for the reign of his son, Henry VIII.

Two Rivers

Throughout the two centuries of unceasing campaigning Newcastle on the Tyne and Durham on the Wear played important roles. Both towns continued to grow in size and importance during the fourteenth and fifteenth centuries and there would have been large bodies of men and supplies constantly moving up the Tyne and over the bridge at Newcastle towards the 'Scottish front' – the Tweed-Solway line.

Durham Cathedral, Castle and Priory were less in the firing line than Newcastle although Norham Castle was part of the Palatine of Durham. Border defences were based around 'Marches' or regions and in Edward II's reign in 1309 the Warden of the Marches became a permanent official of the crown. At first there were two Marches, later three. They existed on both sides of the Border and each was eventually controlled by a Warden who was usually a local magnate. For example on the English side the Percy family held the Middle and East Marches and the Nevilles the West. The Wardens had increasingly powerful positions and with the only permanent force under arms in England they governed the North and answered only to the crown. By the end of the fourteenth century the Scottish and English Wardens were responsible to their respective crowns for the settling of disputes and maintaining law and order.

The Percys were originally from Normandy, settling in Yorkshire immediately after the Conquest. After they purchased Alnwick Castle in 1309 from the Bishop of Durham, Bishop Bek, their rise to power went almost unchallenged for two centuries. By 1377 Richard II had made Henry Percy Earl of Northumberland. At the end of the fourteenth century the Wardens of the Marches were Percy, Earl of Northumberland, Neville, Earl of Westmorland, and Bolingbroke, Duke of Lancaster. These northern magnates had immense power and in 1399 when they combined forces Henry Bolingbroke was able to seize the throne from Richard. During the ensuing Wars of the Roses the Percys supported the Lancastrians and the Nevilles the Yorkists. In the subsequent civil war the Houses of York and Lancaster were almost destroyed but the Percys and Nevilles survived almost intact. These two 'kingmaking' families continued to be a threat to the power of the

Above: Hylton fortified tower house, built about 1400 by Sir William Hylton just north of the River Wear and in the parish of Wearmouth. An early member of the Hylton family 'Romanus de Helton' was charged in 1157 by the Prior of Durham with 'not neglecting St Peter's Church Wearmouth'.

Below: Over the main entrance to the Hylton tower house are carved heraldic shields and the stone banners display the arms of Henry IV and the Hylton family.

crown until they were brought to heel by Henry IV and later Elizabeth I. Newcastle, as a royal castle, was always an important centre from which the king could exert power and control over the northern magnates.

The Scottish and English magnates, especially the Douglas and Percy families, feuded across the Border and battles such as Otterburn were the result of these feuds. Local clansmen on both sides of the Border raided and fought each other in this long and dismal Border warfare. Some English kings, notably Henry VIII, actively encouraged the Wardens

The remains of the fifteenth century chapel at Hylton tower house.

and the English Border clans to raid, even ordering the Earl of Northumberland 'to let slip them of Tynedale and Redesdale for the annoyance of Scotland' and instructing Sir William Percy 'to make a raid at least once a week while the grass is on the ground'. It was not surprising then that the Border clansmen lived and acted outside the law, as poverty and hunger forced them to raid and plunder or 'reive' across the Border for sheep, cattle and horses. Throughout the region in the fourteenth, fifteenth and sixteenth centuries a number of fortified manors and tower houses or 'peles' were built by local landowners for protection against the reivers, despite the increasing use of gunpowder which was making the mighty Norman stone castles vulnerable and eventually militarily obsolete.

Newcastle, although strategically important in the Border wars, was some distance away from the front and as a result suffered less disruptions during the 1300s and 1400s than the towns and villages to the north; so it continued to grow in independence and importance. In 1300 the town was governed by a mayor and four bailiffs. There were problems of corruption and in 1342 Edward III confirmed a charter for the better running of the town. The council, or Corporation, was to be composed of 24 members, the most senior

of the brethren of the twelve 'Mysteries' or leading craft guilds (wool merchants, cloth merchants (mercers), skinners, tailors, saddlers, corn merchants, bakers, tanners, cordwainers, butchers, smiths and fullers). It was a complex, very undemocratic, system of election that favoured the burgesses and was to last for a long time. The town was also forced to keep proper accounts and court records and the town's charters were to be produced and read once a year. In 1400 the burgesses, or more particularly Roger Thornton, obtained an important charter from Henry IV separating the town of Newcastle from the County of Northumberland and obtaining the right to call it the 'County of Newcastle', although the castle continued to be a crown castle. The charter allowed the town to elect its own sheriff and mayor and to hold its own borough courts in the Guildhall.

Roger Thornton is the best known of Newcastle's medieval merchants. He may have been connected to a landed family in Northumberland but, according to tradition, he came to the town penniless. He became a wealthy shipowner dealing in wool, hides and coal before the end of the fourteenth century and between 1400 and 1428 he was mayor on a number of occasions. He represented Newcastle in Henry IV's parliaments and it was

of Tyne', and was known as the Company of Hostmen. The merchants of this guild were expected to entertain or 'host' the visiting merchants, hence its name. Formally established in 1600 by Elizabeth I as the 'Fraternity of Hostmen of Newcastle' the guild had been in existence for at least 100 years as part of the Merchant Adventurers. The tremendous expansion of the coal trade in later centuries gave the Hostmen unprecedented power and influence.

The Prince Bishops of Durham curbed any attempts by local towns and villages to challenge the power of the Palatinate (although they did issue charters to their own boroughs) and determinedly fought Newcastle's growth and expansionism. Anthony Bek was Bishop from 1284 to 1310 and did much to consolidate the power of the Palatinate. He was a fine soldier and supported Edward I's claim to the Scottish throne. He led a section of the English army at Falkirk where William Wallace was defeated but stood against Edward I when the king demanded that the men of the Palatinate do military service beyond the region. Throughout the fourteenth and fifteenth centuries the Bishops continued to collect taxes, mint coins, appoint judges and sheriffs and administer the criminal and ecclesiastical law.

When Newcastle was swept by fire and the bridge destroyed, the new bridge was the joint responsibility of the Newcastle burgesses and the Bishops of Durham. The burgesses fought hard for the right to control all of the bridge but in 1416 Bishop Thomas Langley established his right to the southern section. Bishop Langley was even able to make Parliament recognise the 'princely rights' of the Palatinate between the Tyne and the Wear.

Removed some distance from the 'Scottish front', and throughout the fourteenth and fifteenth centuries, the Prince Bishops of Durham and their communities and small settlements along the River Wear generally prospered. Markets grew and developed (one for example at Wolsingham on the Wear) and in the growing town of Durham, Guilds were created – skinners, salters, mercers and grocers. There were military invasions, notably by King David II of Scotland, that had to be fought by the Prince Bishops, and the Black Death struck in 1349 along the Wear as it did along the Tyne. The region was strongly Lancastrian because of the Neville family, Lords of Raby and Brancepeth Castles, but the settlements along the banks of the River Wear saw little fighting during the Wars of the Roses, unlike the Tyne where a major battle near Hexham gave the Yorkists an important victory that led to the capture of Henry VI.

On the River Tyne and during the sixteenth and seventeenth centuries, Newcastle's power and importance continued to grow as coal mining, trade and industry developed. On the Wear, the Palatinate would begin to lose much of its ecclesiastical privileges. There was however one tiny settlement on the River Wear which was eventually to challenge the industrial might of Newcastle and the world – Sunderland. There is evidence from a Prince Bishop's survey in 1346 that a *'Thomas Menvill occupied a certain place called Hindon, for the building of ships, for which he paid to the bishop an annual rent of 2s'.* This place was to become the 'ship building capital of the world'.

CHAPTER SEVEN

THE AGE OF THE TUDORS:
renaissance, reformation, rebellion and union
(1485-1603)

The Tudor Age (1485-1603) is often considered to be one of Britain's 'golden ages' when the straight-jackets of medieval feudalism and religious orthodoxy were finally discarded. The sixteenth century opened with the English nation becoming increasingly self-confident and assertive, and closed – after centuries of civil and continental warfare – with the formation of a peaceful, powerful and more or less united kingdom.

During the Tudor Age the Renaissance, or rebirth of learning, flowered as the ancient Greek and Roman scholars were rediscovered. Fifteenth and sixteenth century Italian writers, sculptors, painters and architects triggered an intellectual and cultural movement that was to have far-reaching effects throughout the whole of Europe. By the middle of the sixteenth century the Renaissance had reached its peak in northern Europe: the Dutch writer and Christian humanist, Erasmus; the German painter, Durer, and England's Shakespeare stand out as symbols of the art, culture and enlightenment of the period.

The Reformation, the religious movement that started in 1517 when Martin Luther nailed his 95 theses on the castle church at Wittenburg, swept through sixteenth century Europe. Initially it was simply a means of reforming the Roman Catholic church but, as the Reformation gathered momentum, it led to a violent political struggle for the French crown, the bloody wars of Independence of the Netherlands against colonial Spain and the birth of the independent Protestant church which indirectly was to bring about the union of Scotland and England. Henry VIII broke with the Roman Catholic church and in Scotland John Knox had a great influence on the Scottish Reformation which led, in the 1590s, to the birth of the Presbyterian movement and, in 1599, to the final break down of the 'Auld Alliance' of Scotland and

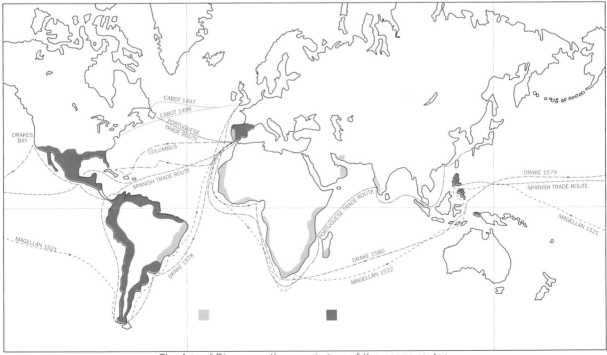

The Age of Discovery: the opening up of the ocean routes.

Carracks and Galleons. Carracks were the new, three masted deep sea traders that rapidly appeared around 1400 and would have entered the Tyne. Galleons were the supreme sixteenth century ocean traders and the English galleons played an important role in defeating the 1588 Armada.

France. Peace between Scotland and England was secured when Protestant James VI came to the throne in Scotland in 1567 and to the English throne in 1603 as James I.

One of the major effects of the Hundred Years War (1337-1453) with France had been the growth of an English national identity. The French and Latin languages were finally discarded as English became the tongue of the aristocrats, poets and playwrights. The sixteenth century produced some of the finest English-language playwrights and poets that the world has ever known.

During the Hundred Years War, Welsh and English longbow archers had shattered the nobility of Europe with their cloth-yard arrows and, with the invention of gunpowder and cannon ball, the castle walls of the feudal lords

could be brought to ruin in a matter of hours. Caxton's printing press further undermined the monopoly of learning exerted throughout the ages by the literate clergy and the more sophisticated courtiers. Henry VIII's Reformation resulted in the rejection of the authority of the Roman Catholic Church with Henry, rather than the Pope, as the Head of the English Church. The Reformation also completed the decline of the medieval role of the monks and friars in English society when the Monasteries were dissolved in the 1530s and their treasures taken by the Crown.

Columbus' Voyage of Discovery in 1492 heralded the great 'Age of Discovery'. Initially it was the Spanish and Portuguese who opened up the New World but it was not long before Drake had circumnavigated the world and the

Early sixteenth century chart of Britain and western Europe showing three masted ocean traders and Scotland separated from England!

English 'Merchant Adventurers' were voyaging overseas. They explored and traded in carracks, their newly-evolved, three-masted, sailing ships: overseas trade was soon to become of vital importance to the British economy. Ships had been growing in size throughout the fifteenth century and more masts had been added. Henry VIII built a magnificent four-masted sailing ship, the *Grace a Dieu*, with a revolutionary design – gun ports cut into the hull. The cannon 'broadside' was to come of age and be used with devastating effect by the English against the Spanish Armada in 1588.

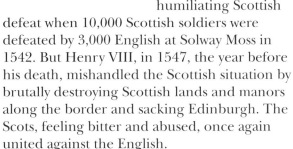

During the sixteenth century there was a general decline in the power of the nobility and an increasing emancipation of the serf, faster in the

Henry VIII (1509-1547).

south than in the more feudal north. The dramatic growth of trade, both national and international, led to the growth of a wealthy merchant or bourgeois class – the middle class. Throughout the century, trade expanded between villages and chartered towns and, of ever increasing importance, the wool and cloth manufacturing trade extended to cottages and farms throughout England and Wales.

Land continued to be fenced in or enclosed to make its use more efficient. But enclosures were a constant cause of strife between landlord and tenants especially when, without prior agreement, the landlords fenced off land where the peasant had had grazing rights for centuries. A series of Acts were passed in the sixteenth century preventing enclosures but they were less and less effective.

The two much vaunted monarchs of the Tudor Age were Henry VIII (King, 1509-1547) and Elizabeth I (Queen, 1558-1603). Both monarchs were despotic, although more or less popular, with Henry VIII becoming especially tyrannical in the declining years of his 36-year-long reign.

Once the joys of sport and hedonism had been indulged, Henry VIII was hungry for power and possessions. He invaded France and won the battle of the Spurs in 1513. Scotland, which was allied to France by James IV of Scotland, took an opportunity to invade England but was smashed by Henry's northern army in 1513 at Flodden Field with the Bishop of Durham supplying a large army and the English fighting under the banner of St Cuthbert. In the fight the Scottish king was killed along with three bishops, eleven earls, fifteen lords and some 10,000 men. A second English invasion was attempted by James V (son of James IV and married to the King of France's daughter Madeline) and it too ended in an humiliating Scottish defeat when 10,000 Scottish soldiers were defeated by 3,000 English at Solway Moss in 1542. But Henry VIII, in 1547, the year before his death, mishandled the Scottish situation by brutally destroying Scottish lands and manors along the border and sacking Edinburgh. The Scots, feeling bitter and abused, once again united against the English.

Henry VIII, once a devout Catholic, had a major impact on the evolution of the British nation when he broke with Rome so as to divorce his brother's widow, Catherine of Aragon, and marry his already pregnant mistress Anne Boleyn. Arthur, Henry VIII's eldest brother and the son of Henry VII and Elizabeth of York, was prematurely born, stunted and sickly. He was married in his early teens to Catherine, the daughter of King Ferdinand and Queen Isabella of Spain, as part of the Tudor's attempt to balance power in Europe. Arthur died of 'sweating sickness' in Ludlow castle in the Welsh Marches and, in order to continue the strategic alliance with Spain, Henry VII promptly married his youngest son Henry VIII to Catherine.

In 1534 Henry VIII's confidant and minister, Thomas Cromwell, carried legislation through an obedient parliament to make Henry head of the English church and to sever all links with the Pope. Henry married Anne Boleyn and set about 'dissolving the monasteries' so as to break the allegiance of the abbots and priors with their titular heads outside Henry's domain. The dissolution of the monasteries gave him vast tracts of land and the forfeited monastic treasures gave the crown treasury, which was short of funds, an important injection of capital. The confiscated land gave him an enormous, free, source of patronage with which to influence and pacify the gentry. Everyone in Tudor England, from commoner to magnate, was hungry for land. By giving away or selling off the lands of the dissolved monasteries and friaries to the lesser lords, knights and richer merchants, Henry brought about a substantial redistribution of wealth in England which tended to favour the developing middle classes. But the dissolution of the monasteries was not without problems. It led, in part, to rebellion in the feudal, Catholic north in 1537 – the Pilgrimage of Grace – which Henry put down with much violence.

Throughout his reign Henry VIII was equally revengeful with both Catholics and Protestants – they only had to disagree with his policies – but his church reforms unleashed Protestantism so that much of the latter part of his reign was taken up with attempts to hold it back, along with attempts to deal with the continuing wars with France and Scotland. Besides destroying the medieval power of the Roman Catholic church tin England and Wales, probably Henry VIII's other most important act was to create the English Royal Navy. On his death his willed succession (Edward, Mary, Elizabeth) took place.

Edward VI (King, 1547-1553) became King when he was only 10 years old but power was held by the Protector, the Duke of Somerset, until 1550 when the Duke of Northumberland seized power. During the 'reign' of Edward VI, himself a devout Protestant, the Protestant Reformation made much progress.

Mary I ('Bloody Mary', Queen, 1553-1558), a devout Catholic, was unable to lastingly return the English church and people back to the Pope (the Counter Reformation) despite repealing Henry VIII's and Edward VI's Protestant legislation, reintroducing the heresy laws and burning 300 Protestant martyrs at the stake. She married Philip II of Spain in 1554.

Elizabeth was the daughter of Henry VIII by his second wife, Anne Boleyn. Elizabeth was well educated by tutors, well versed in the new Renaissance learning and could speak many languages. She sided with her half sister Mary on the death of Edward VI in 1553 against Lady Jane Grey and the Duke of Northumberland who tried to secure the succession by marrying Jane against her wishes to his son. Lady Jane was Queen for nine days in 1553 but, because she lacked popular support, was forced to abdicate in favour of Mary I. Lady Jane was imprisoned in the Tower of London and beheaded in 1554. Elizabeth's apparent pro-Protestant position made her unpopular with Mary I who imprisoned Elizabeth for her supposed support of a rebellion led by Thomas Wyatt.

Elizabeth I (1558-1603).

Elizabeth I succeeded on Mary's death in 1558. Elizabeth was not a devout Protestant but recognised the political expediency of aligning herself with the Protestant nations in Europe against Catholic Scotland, and further that she had to be very wary of the powerful, Catholic continental states of France and Spain. Despite many 'affairs of the heart' the 'Virgin Queen' refused to marry.

The natural heir to Elizabeth's throne was the Catholic Mary, Queen of Scots, daughter of James V of Scotland and a French noblewoman, Mary of Guise. Mary lived in the French court and married Francis II of France. He died and Mary returned to Scotland where she married Lord Darnley and subsequently gave birth to James VI of Scotland (later James I of England). She clashed with the Scottish nobles and, with her armies defeated and her son declared King of Scotland by the nobles, she fled to England were she remained, under constraint, for some 20 years before being finally executed by Elizabeth. During those 20 years Mary was the focal point for all dissident English Catholics and the centre of many Catholic plots against Elizabeth but it was not until 1586, when the Spanish Armada and possible invasion loomed, that Elizabeth signed her death warrant. Henry's creation of the English Royal Navy was well vindicated when, in 1588, the Spanish Armada was destroyed by the English galleons of Lord Howard of Effingham and buccaneers like Hawkins and Drake. The long-lasting Scottish Border warfare gradually subsided in Elizabeth's reign as Protestant James VI of Scotland was expected to succeed her as England's next king (James I of England).

Throughout the Tudor period 'the state' was still very much 'the crown' and the Parliament the servant of the crown. Parliament was increasingly involved in the decision-making process as the English population grew and business and trade expanded. The emerging European nations clashed and, as British government became more complex, Parliament played a dual role in the Tudor Age as both debating chamber and law maker.

Through much of the sixteenth century the population grew but did not outstrip the country's resources as it had in the fourteenth century before the Black Death. By 1600 the population had recovered to over four million. But the north, compared to the south, was far poorer and much less populated and not yet fully recovered from the 'Harrying of the North' and the 'dread pestilence'. It was also suffering from the debilitating effect of centuries of border warfare and the people and much of the land were controlled by the powerful northern magnates.

Two Rivers

The Scottish Border Wars continued for a good part of the sixteenth century with the English magnates, the Earls of Northumberland and Westmorland (the powerful Catholic Percy and Neville families) commanding virtual standing armies often as Wardens of the Marches. When Henry VIII severed links with the Pope and declared himself head of the English Church he rightly saw the earls as a threat, especially the staunchly Catholic Percy family. The earl's retainer system had severely limited the crown's authority throughout much of the medieval period so he created the 'Crown Party' where, in return for military service on the border, the gentry were offered a retainer by the state rather than by an earl.

Henry further reasserted royal authority in the north when, in 1537, the massive estates of the debt-laden, 'unthrifty' sixth Earl of Northumberland were taken over by the state and, following the dissolution, he enormously curtailed the power and influence of the Prince Bishops of Durham by an Act of Parliament that curtailed the Palatine's right to administer criminal justice, mint coins, collect taxes and appoint sheriffs and judges. The Bishop's courts were still used but there was a clear break in that the Crown was now the head of the judicial process within the Palatine.

Henry set about dissolving the lesser monasteries in 1536. In Newcastle the five friaries and the nunnery were taken over and their lands sold to the Corporation, rich merchants and gentry with most of their precious vestments going to the crown treasury. It was not surprising that Henry VIII's actions against the church and their power caused the catholic and feudalistic northern magnates to rebel. They did so twice: once in his reign in 1536 – the Pilgrimage of Grace – and again in Elizabeth's reign in 1569 – the Rising of the Northern Earls.

The Pilgrimage of Grace was also popular among the monks suffering from the effects of the dissolution as well as among the commoners, upset by unscrupulous new landlords who were enclosing their traditional grazing lands, and many of the out-of-work earls' retainers. Together they formed a well-equipped, well-led army of some 30,000 men and marched south to meet the Duke of Norfolk, who commanded a much smaller

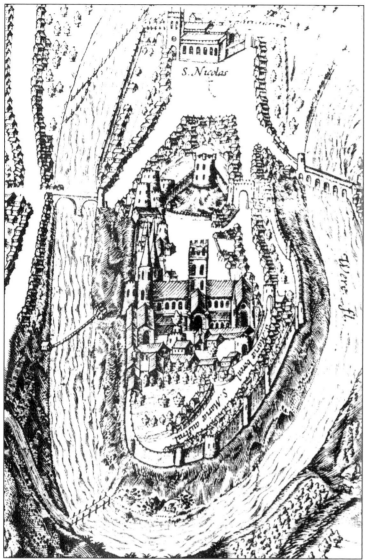

Durham about 1590.

government's main administrative agent for the north. Durham monastery, for long the intellectual centre of the north under its Benedictine monks, was dissolved in 1539. The Cathedral shrines of St Cuthbert and the Venerable Bede were defaced and valuables stripped from the high altar but Durham was allowed to keep its Bishop. Although the abbey was dissolved, the building was not destroyed and the Prior became a Dean to the cathedral. The merchants of Durham lost much of their brisk pilgrim trade which was centred round the shrines of Cuthbert, Bede and Oswald.

The 'Rising of the Earls' in Elizabeth's reign was the last attempt of the Neville and Percy families to win back their feudal, once 'kingmaking', powers. Catholic Queen Mary had revived the Percy fortunes by giving the earldom to the Catholic nephew of 'Percy the unthrifty' whose estates had been taken over by the crown. The Rising was precipitated by Mary Queen of Scots' arrival at Workington in 1568 and her subsequent detention in Bolton Castle by Elizabeth. In the following year the Catholic earls of Westmorland, Charles Neville, and Northumberland, Thomas Percy, took a force to Durham Cathedral

force of some 8,000 men. At Pontefract the rebel army disbanded after a 'Parliament of the North' agreed to their demands. The leaders of the Pilgrimage were given a King's Pardon and two were allowed to place their grievances (which included the reunion of the English Church with Rome and the restoration of the powers of the Bishop Princes) before Henry at Windsor. Promises were made but a second rising in the following year allowed Henry to break his word and extract a vicious vengeance: the leaders were executed and men were hung in batches at, for example, Carlisle, Durham and York.

In 1537 Henry used the 'Council of the North' to further inhibit the power of the northern earls and Palatine. The Council immediately took over the judicial rights that once belonged to the Wardens and the Prince Bishops and became, eventually, the

where they ripped up the new English Bible and conducted a Catholic mass before going on to besiege Barnard Castle where its owner, Sir George Bowes, was loyal to Elizabeth. Although the castle surrendered, the Earls were unable to sustain their uprising and fled to Scotland, but the Protestant Scottish Regent handed Percy over to Elizabeth. With Percy's beheading and the attainder of Neville, the feudal power of the Nevilles and Percys was finally destroyed. The Earl of Northumberland's brother was allowed to keep Alnwick Castle by declaring that he was a Protestant, but he was later imprisoned and subsequently died mysteriously in the Tower of London. Border warfare gradually died out during Elizabeth's reign and the rapid growth of the coal industry offered some employment to many of the unemployed retainers of the northern magnates.

As the Tudor Kings, Queens and magnates fought to establish their power bases, the new merchant classes on the Tyne and, to a far lesser extent the Wear, fought for theirs. One indirect effect of Henry VIII's dissolution of the monasteries was to bring to an end, in Newcastle's favour, its long-running struggle with Tynemouth and Durham Priories for the control of the Tyne. The Duke of Northumberland, when governing for Edward VI, even went as far as to allow Newcastle to

The Ostmen's seal. Although formally established in 1600 the Fraternity of Hostmen of Newcastle had already been in existence for at least 100 years.

annex Gateshead as a 'suburb' of Newcastle, although Mary I reunited 'the manor' with the restored Bishopric of Durham.

The powerful merchant class grew as national and international trade improved and the authority of the feudal magnates and the Prince Bishops of Durham declined. Edward Baxter was a Merchant Adventurer, the Tudor equivalent of Roger Thornton (page 63) and, like Thornton, four times mayor of Newcastle. Baxter belonged to an elite class of merchants, the Merchant Adventurers, whose guilds were established in the town sometime before 1480 to trade exclusively and mainly in wool, grain and cloth (mercery) and later timber, wood and, of course, coal. The

Merchant Adventurers fought long and hard for Newcastle's, and their, trading rights and cartels.

Edward Baxter had multiple interests. He shipped wool, lead and hides to the continent and acted as an 'Ostman' for coal shipments from the Tyne, specialising in hosting (page 75) coal for vessels from northern France. Another contemporary of Baxter was Lewes Sotheran who was also a Hostman as well as a shipowner and master mariner. When Henry VIII went to war with France in the early part of his reign he needed merchant ships to be fitted out for naval service. Newcastle supplied two: Sotheran owned both of them, and he even commanded one of them, *Elizabeth*, in the royal navy's ill-fated attack on the French fleet in Brest in 1513.

From the middle of the fifteenth to the middle of the sixteenth century the volume of exports from Newcastle rose five-fold, mostly due to the export of coal, a high volume cargo, and most of the cargo was carried in small ships of under 100 tons. In 1558, when Elizabeth was crowned, there were some 60 Newcastle-owned vessels, with a total weight of 4000 tons, or an average weight of 66.7 tons per ship.

The Dissolution, or 'Capitalist Reformation' as it is sometimes known, had an enormous effect on the future economy of the Tyne and the Wear for it allowed the Merchant Adventurers unfettered access to the coal mines that had previously been leased by Tynemouth and Durham Priories with the restrictively high rents and limited output. Tynemouth Priory, for example, leased out the Elswick mines in 1530 and limited output to 31 tons a day, while Elizabeth's lease imposed no restrictions on output.

There was an ever increasing demand for coal during the Tudor Age. Wood as a fuel, a cooking and a building material was becoming in short supply as towns, especially London, grew in size. Forests were decimated to build the expanding (both in tonnage and number) Royal and merchant navies. The North East could meet the demand for there was a plentiful supply of readily accessible coal in the rich, northern coalfields.

Nevertheless coal was capital intensive and a risky business and enormous profits could be lost as well as made. It could only be shipped in the summer months; it had to be stockpiled in the winter and building staithes and sinking shafts cost vast amounts of money. William Gray, whose history of Newcastle was printed in 1649, wrote: *'One coale merchant imployeth 500... or a thousand in his works of coale; yet for all his labour, care, and cost, can scarce live of his trade, nay many of them hath consumed and spent great estates, and dyed beggers'*. The tightly knit Hostmen, with their cartel and control of the Tyne, controlled the coal production business. They had capital and economies of scale on their side and few coal entrepreneurs survived if they were not members of the Company of Hostmen.

In 1583 Queen Elizabeth leased the important group of ex-Palatinate mines of Gateshead and Whickham to two Newcastle merchants who apportioned them to the leading Hostmen. These were extremely wealthy pits, producing 100,000 tons of coal a year by the end of the 1600s. It was not surprising that the expressions 'colles to Newcastell' was first coined about then and Tyneside became known as the 'Black Indies'. New pits were dug at, for example, Ryton, Winlaton and Stella and, with the development of new pumping techniques, older pits were opened up and deepened – the Gateshead pits were now over 200ft deep. In 1603, Londoners complained about the increase in the price of 'sea cole ' and the wily, cartel-holding Hostmen gave the excuse that the deeper pits and the increase in distance from the newly sunk pits to the river disembarking points, or staithes, was the cause of the price increase.

Coal exports from the Tyne dramatically increased from about 15,000 tons a year in the late 1500s to 400,000 tons by the first quarter of the seventeenth century. Towards the very end of Elizabeth's reign Huntingdon Beaumont, a very early North East mining engineer, built the first wooden railways at Bedlington, Cowpen and Bebside where horses pulled coal wagons on wooden rails, forerunners of the mining engineering revolution that was to occur on Tyneside.

In 1600 Elizabeth granted Newcastle a charter that allowed an exclusive body of electors (mainly the Hostmen) the right to elect the mayor and burgesses of the town. The town was given to the mayor and the burgesses with an annual fee farm (page 55) of £100 and the Common Council of the town was to be made up of the sheriff, 10 aldermen and 24 burgesses who had the right to make bylaws. The town's independence and power were further strengthened when Newcastle's sheriffs and mayors were given the right to build gallows (which were constructed outside the West Gate) and hold regular meetings of the town's court. This charter officially incorporated the Company of Hostmen and the new Grammar School (whose teachers were appointed by the Hostmen). The charter also gave the Hostmen the exclusive right to load coal at any point on the Tyne. Within a month of the issuing of the charter the Hostmen *'in gratitude for their incorporation'* agreed to pay the crown one shilling for every chaldron of coal shipped out of the Tyne. Thanks to the charter the Hostmen were now, officially, the Newcastle power brokers' and they continued to exercise their long-held power: with one exception every mayor from 1600 to 1640 was a 'Lord of Coal', that is an important member of the Company of Hostmen.

In Elizabeth's reign, Newcastle's population was probably around 10,000. The mayor and the members of the Corporation did not always act out of self-interest and decided to make themselves responsible for the town's water supply and sanitation and to take measures to deal with plague and flu or the 'sweating sickness' as it was then known. Black Death continued to visit the town, in 1579, 1589, 1595 and 1597, and it was not uncommon for over a tenth of Newcastle's population to be carried off in an outbreak. Plague, coupled with bad harvests, resulted in famine, unrest and finally riot, with attempts by the artisans to broaden the base of local government and break the power of the rich merchants. But the rioters had little success; Elizabeth's 1600 royal charter had institutionalised the Company of Hostmen's powerful control over the town's economic and municipal life.

In Elizabeth's reign the Tyne was becoming a busy river. There were some 300 ships involved in the coastal trade and ships from many different countries visited the port of Newcastle. In 1536 Henry VIII had granted a guild of pilots and mariners. The guild was originally a religious fraternity, the Guild of the Blessed Trinity, which was closely associated with All Saints' Church. The guild was allowed

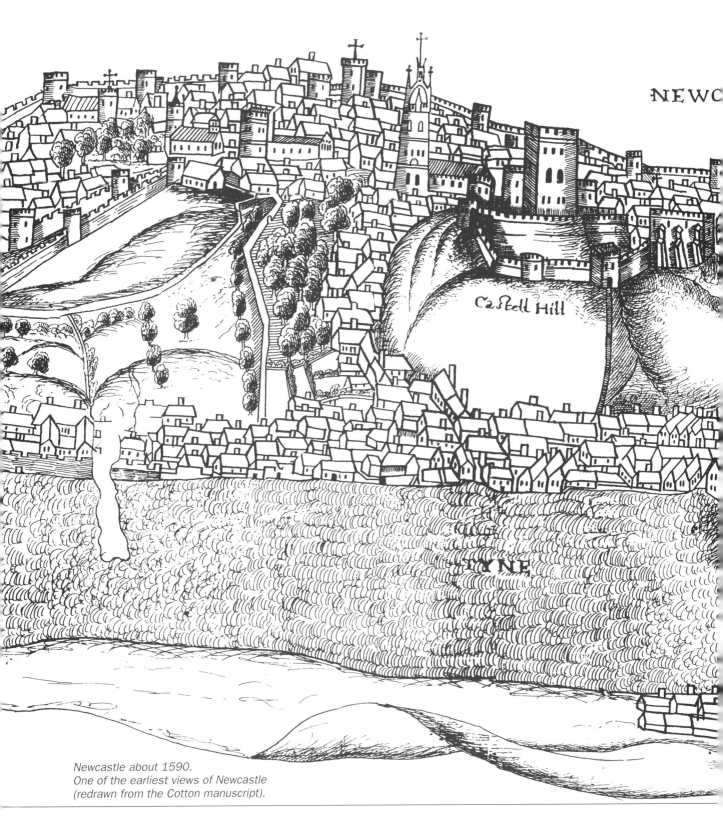

NEWC

Ca∫tell Hill

TYNE

Newcastle about 1590.
One of the earliest views of Newcastle
(redrawn from the Cotton manuscript).

to build two leading lights at North Shields, lit by candles, to help ships navigate the dangerous entrance of the Tyne and the lights were, according to tradition, built from stone from the dissolved Newcastle friaries. The guild was refounded under Elizabeth as the Master, Pilots and Seamen of the Trinity House of Newcastle upon Tyne. In 1606 they were granted a further charter which defined the fees they could levy on ships entering or leaving the Tyne. But it was the Hostmen who, once again, had final control, for Charles I granted the mayor and burgesses (ie. the Hostmen) of Newcastle total jurisdiction within the port of Tyne, which extended from 'Hedwine Streames to a place in the sea called the Sparhawke', a region which was more or less the tidal Tyne.

So successfully did the Hostmen exploit their Elizabethan monopolies that they were able to refer to South Shields, at the mouth of the Tyne, as 'a station for our coal fleet'. But, independently tfd Newcastle and during the 1500s and 1600s, North and South Shields had been developing a profitable sea salt industry. Before the use of ice in the late eighteenth century salting and smoking were the only

means of preserving meat and fish and the sea-salt industries on the lower reaches of the Tyne (and Wear) were important local industries until the discovery of land-based salt deposits.

Since 1225 Tynemouth Priory had been developing a fishing port on the north bank of the Tyne at North Shields to replace the 'shiels' or simple huts that were used by the earlier fishermen. Salt for pickling the fish came from the sea. South Shields had gradually built up its salt-making industry and, at high tide, sea water was piped in from the Tyne and 'salters' would evaporate the brine using coal fires lit under huge flat pans that at first were made of lead and later, in the 1400s, of iron. By the mid-1500s there were some 200 salt pans in both North and South Shields and the industry employed many salters and keelmen who brought the coal downstream from the up-river mines. In the 1600s, North Sea fishing vessels would arrive in their hundreds to load salt, but the industry declined in the mid-1700s when coal became more expensive and the natural salt deposits were discovered in Cheshire.

During the fifteenth century the belligerent Newcastle burgesses demanded, much to the displeasure of the South Shields men, that ships could only be worked at Newcastle. They even complained to the Bishop of Durham that he had built *'a town at South Shields where no town should be!'* During Henry VIII's reign there were complaints from the Newcastle burgesses that the Prior of Tynemouth was daily loading and discharging ships at Tynemouth and Shields thereby robbing the crown of its dues. Further the Prior was making *'fyschgarths (fish traps) and weeres for takyn salmone'* between Newcastle and the sea and each year moved them from place to place so that the port was *'wrekked and shallowed'*. In 1529 a statute was passed decreeing that within the tidal limits of the Tyne all goods had to be loaded at Newcastle. The statute was only slightly modified by the 1600 royal charter which

allowed ships, if they were too large to sail up the Tyne to Newcastle, to load and unload at the river's mouth. This is one of the earliest references to the increasing shallowness of the Tyne and an indication that Shields was becoming an important harbour.

The Wear remained largely unexploited and its mouth difficult to navigate through much of the Tudor Age. In 1588 a Queen Elizabeth Commission, investigating the apparent lack of custom dues from the town, reported that there was no Custom House. But there were coal workings and salt pans and Sunderland was a fishing village of 30 householders. There was no sign of Menvill's shipbuilding industry (page 65) and only 20 fishermen were there working seven cobles. The town was said to be in 'great decay' and 'little frequented'.

But, as at Shields on the Tyne, cheap local coal could be profitably employed to produce salt. In 1589 a Robert Bowes of Biddick set up a serious salt making enterprise at Sunderland at 'The Pans', piping in the brine from the Wear to salt pans that were 20ft square and 6ft deep. It was a success and some 40 years later the Sunderland salt pans were producing some 50,000 baskets of salt annually. Bowes also owned a coal pit at Offerton from which he extracted coal for the pans. There were other Wearsiders who were taking an interest in coal mining, notably the Lambtons and Lumleys, but although keels were bringing coal down to the ships at the river mouth there was nothing like the same degree of activity as there was on the Tyne. This was to change in the Civil War.

CHAPTER EIGHT

THE CIVIL WARS: fortress, fuel and trade
(1600-1658)

The first half of the seventeenth century, until Oliver Cromwell's death in 1658, saw some of the most dramatic and eventful years of British history: a monarch was publicly beheaded; England became a republic; there was rule by a dictator; the roots were laid for parliamentary ascendancy over the Crown and there was an unprecedented expansion in national and international trade. By 1600 the Age of Discovery was more or less over and great progress had been made in opening up the trade wind routes in the Atlantic and Indian Oceans. Despite the failure of the Spanish Armadas (there were more than one) and the naval supremacy of the Elizabethan galleon, Spain was still the major power in Europe and Philip II of Spain was still bent on conquering England and had severely curtailed English trade. Holland, who had pioneered the building of cheap, unarmed merchantmen (such as the *fluyts*), had the monopoly of the trade in the North and Baltic Seas. As the century progressed all was to change.

The Renaissance from 1400 to 1600 had led to the development and refinement of the three-masted ocean trader, cartography, celestial navigation and the cannon, and Englishmen were abroad and trading in ever increasing numbers. Their early obsession with silver, gold and spices was replaced with a desire for coffee, tea, muslin, silk, sugar and slaves. Powerful trading companies worked the seas and England's merchant ships competed with those of France, Sweden and Holland. The trading companies developed private armies and navies and the English government eventually had to use legislation to curb the power of the 'Honourable East India Company' which created a monopoly of trade with India and China. Between 1618 and 1620 there was open war between the English and the Dutch trading companies in the East. Around England's shores coastal traders were working in ever increasing numbers, supplying the growing town of London with goods and

especially the new and important fuel – coal. The English coastal trade was to greatly benefit from the wars with Holland as large numbers of Dutch coastal merchantmen were taken as prizes.

Throughout the seventeenth century there were bloody struggles ashore and on the oceans as Britain competed with the other empire-building nations, Portugal, Spain, France, Holland. As one country fell another rose to take its place. England the aggressor built up her Royal Navy and fought for domination with Spain, (1624-30, 1655-60), France (1627-30), and Holland, (1651-54, 1665-67, 1672-74). The prize to the victor was trade and colonies. Sir Walter Raleigh summarised the situation: '*Whosoever commands the sea commands trade; whosoever commands the trade of the world commands the riches of the world, and consequently the world itself*'. The first English colonists arrived in 1607 in America in Chesapeake Bay and by the 1650s there were colonies in Massachusetts, Maryland and Virginia.

Holland rose to power in the late sixteenth and early seventeenth century as a result of the activities of its merchants and a government which creatively backed colonial growth, sea trade, investment and banking. England and Holland clashed and after three Anglo-Dutch wars, by the end of the seventeenth century, England began to overtake Holland to emerge as one of the most powerful maritime nations.

Elizabeth encouraged trading companies, granting a charter to the London East India Company in 1600. When she died in 1603 the Tudors had done much: unified Britain; instigated the Reformation; defeated religious extremism; developed a Royal Navy; beaten off Spain; overseen an increasingly assertive Parliament; and helped English merchants and seamen to play an active role in the worldwide expansion of trade.

Both the Tudors and Stuarts reigned over Britain's longest period of domestic peace which lasted from 1570 until the outbreak of the first Civil War and during this period, especially the earlier part, there had been unprecedented growth and a consolidation of the merchant and middle classes. The rich merchants of the towns bought up manors and land (often a result of the Dissolution) and became part of the 'gentry', a term which included the country gentry or squires. Rich town merchants, with their lavish town houses, became part of the new, 'landless gentry'. It was the local gentry who were responsible for disseminating the will of government through local courts, Justices of the Peace or borough aldermen who were often Justices of the Peace. In the towns it was corporations, usually self perpetuating oligarchies (as exemplified by the Hostmen of Newcastle), who exerted the king's power.

The aristocracy, the great landowners, were also part of the administrative system. The gentry sent representatives to Parliament, the peers went to the House of Lords, and both houses – the Lords and the Commons – were, by the beginning of the seventeenth century, recognised constituents of government. But the Crown was still the head and power of government and Parliament was subservient to the Crown and the Privy Council, the important advisory body to the Crown. The Crown ruled as long as there was a common interest in goals between Privy Council and the peers, the town aldermen and the country gentry. The Privy Council was an important body that had grown out of the King's Court (Curia Regis) where the king once consulted with the nobles. The various other bodies such as the Council of the North, the Court of Star Chamber, the Court of High Commission and so on were all extensions of the royal authority. These prerogative bodies existed because of the Crown and, as both councils and courts, they had procedures that administered justice, for example, far more quickly than the Common Law courts. The coincidence of interest between Crown and town, Crown and country worked well for the Tudors and for the Stuarts during the early part of the seventeenth century. But with England at peace with itself with a recognised law, order and stability, the emergent middle classes, especially the Common Law lawyers, were often keen to limit the discretionary powers of the monarch.

Elizabeth was succeeded by James I in 1603, (King of England 1603-1625; King of Scotland, as James VI, 1567-1625) the first of the Stuart monarchs, and later by his heir Charles I. James I believed in the 'divine rights of kings' and for one period ruled without summoning Parliament for ten years. Likewise his son Charles I dissolved parliament for 11 years and ruled with the help of Thomas Wentworth and Archbishop Laud. Nevertheless, James I (a Protestant King with three Crowns: England, Scotland and Ireland) accepted that he had to make laws and raise taxes through Parliament even though it met and disbanded at his command. The extent to which the Parliament was answerable to the Crown was one of the major reasons for the Civil Wars (1642-51) in Charles' reign.

James I was known as 'the wisest fool in Christendom' as he had much theoretical knowledge, writing a number of books on politics, but little common sense. He sponsored the 'authorised version' of the Bible but through much of his reign he was under the influence of Robert Carr and George Villiers, the Duke of Buckingham. He reversed Elizabeth's policy towards Spain, attempted and failed to achieve a Spanish marriage for his son Charles and, to appease Spain, agreed to Sir Walter Raleigh's execution on a trumped-up charge in 1618. His court was sexually lax and corrupt. Throughout his reign he was short of troops and money which he raised by selling monopolies, benevolences and 'baronetcies' – a title he created.

His son's succession went smoothly and Charles I's reign (King 1625-1649) was in many ways opposite to his father's. Unapproachable, precise, fussy, yet literate and a great connoisseur of art, he presided over a chaste court and made successful attempts to balance the financial affairs of the country. He married the Catholic Henrietta Maria, daughter of the King of France, which made him unpopular with England's growing Puritanical movement which was made up of English Protestants who believed that the Tudor Reformation had not created a 'pure' enough Church. He went unsuccessfully to war with Spain and France. His first three Parliaments underfunded these overseas campaigns so he resorted to unpopular and illegal means by forcing loans and raising taxes from the English people. In 1628, in return for Parliamentary funds, he grudgingly accepted the passing of the 'Petition of Rights' which outlawed his fund raising methods. Parliament was vociferously unhappy about Charles I's unsuccessful

Civil War: Royalist Newcastle

Continental wars, his support for non-Anglican clergy and the general illegality of his tax raising methods. Unable to work with Parliament, Charles dissolved it in 1629 for 11 years ruling through courts and councils.

Without parliament he raised taxes (including the unpopular Ship Money to build the Royal Navy from 1634) and on the whole, during a period of booming foreign trade, successfully ran the country, even managing to balance the budget. But Charles' religious advisor Archbishop Laud, and Laud's religious reforms, were extremely unpopular. Laud tried to impose a religious conformity on the nation, based around the 1559 Prayer Book. Further he set about reinstating the hierarchical power of the Church by insisting that it be governed by bishops (episcopy), thereby upsetting many people and incensing all Puritans. Scotland especially rejected Laud's attempts to force the Scottish Presbyterian Church into an Anglican strait-jacket. Civil disorder grew and in 1638 the 'Covenant with God' swept Scotland as aristocrat and labourer swore allegiance to the Presbyterian Church and God. Charles attempted to impose his will by force. The Scots resisted, mobilised and in order to raise money Charles was forced to recall Parliament – the 'Short Parliament'. But rather than do a deal with Parliament and accept restrictions to the power of the Crown in return for Parliament's promise to raise money, Charles attempted to raise troops by forming alliances with Catholic Spain, the Pope, Irish and Highland Catholics. His attempts all failed. The Scots, in the so-called 'Bishops' War' (1639-1640), invaded England and occupied Newcastle in 1640 (see below).

Desperately short of money Charles called the 'Long Parliament'. Within a year most of the courts and councils that Charles had ruled by were dismantled, with his reluctant agreement, by Parliament. The Privy Council's judicial powers were restricted and the Crown was unable to raise taxes. The MPs, concerned that Charles would unravel these changes, pushed ahead in the Long Parliament with even more radical legislation demanding Parliament's right to appoint and dismiss members of the Privy Council and that the Privy Council and the King be answerable to Parliamentary scrutiny. Suspected by many of his mainly non-Catholic subjects of being a Catholic, Charles' unpopularity was increased when Catholics started slaughtering Protestants

in Ireland and further increased when he unwisely, and unsuccessfully, attempted to arrest five of the leading opposition members of the House of Commons. A thwarted Charles could take no more and, in 1642, raised his standard at Nottingham and declared war on Parliament – the first English Civil War (1642-1646) had begun.

Englishmen were forced to take sides, although some contrived to avoid doing so. For many it was a difficult decision, often a religious one. The King's appeal was mainly two-fold: to those who sympathised with the Church of England or Anglican system, with its Prayer Book, and episcopy; and also to the Roman Catholics, whose religion Charles had treated sympathetically. Parliament's cause appealed to the Puritans who heartily distrusted the Catholics.

London, with its wealth, the home of the Navy and large reserves of manpower, was Parliament's base, while the North and West were the King's. Both sides had similar weapons and tactics and the war of attrition, which it became, was won by Parliament as it was better able to finance its war effort and pay its army. The Royalists had the first limited successes but soon Parliamentary victories followed, especially at the battle of Marston Moor in 1644, where a one-time MP, Oliver Cromwell, displayed his military skill. A year later, the Parliamentary army, 'remodelled' under Cromwell, defeated the Royalists at Naseby. Charles was pursued until he gave himself up to the Scots at Newark a year later. The Scots had entered the war on the side of Parliament in 1644, after being promised legislation favouring the formation of a Presbyterian Scottish Church, which was based on the belief that the highest order in the Church was the Presbyters or Elders who were all of equal rank. The Scots took Charles to Newcastle were he was held for nine months before being handed over to Parliament.

But Charles' surrender and the end of the first Civil War brought little change for most English people. During the war Parliament had ruthlessly taxed them to raise money and even tried to replace Laud's religious dictates with a national, Presbyterian system similar to that in Scotland. The army was powerful enough to control Parliament even getting it to vote for taxes to support the army. Charles I's captivity at Newcastle was not strict and, in an attempt to play off the Scots against the English, he

Seventeenth century engraving of a fluyt at anchor. Hundreds of fluyts, the seventeenth century home trader par excellence, were seized by the English after winning the First Dutch War (1652-1654).

formed an alliance with Scotland which changed sides as they were concerned that Parliament's view of the English Church was not the same as theirs. Charles also gained support from many who believed that the new military rulers were worse than the Crown. The Second English Civil War (1646-1648) followed with rebellions against Parliament occurring spasmodically throughout the country and usually in regions where there had been no previous fighting. But the uprisings were not coordinated and the army, under its increasingly puritanical leader Oliver Cromwell, picked off the rebel districts one by one. Cromwell defeated the Scots at Preston in 1648 to end the second Civil War. Again nothing was solved. The army commanders took control, purged Parliament of Royalists and moderates by arresting or expelling from the House over half of its members and, in 1649, with the Parliament firmly under its control put the King on trial. He refused to recognise Parliament's jurisdiction and was

publicly beheaded. Charles I became a martyr and England became a Republic.

From 1649 to 1653 England was governed by the 'Rump Parliament', the purged remains of the Long Parliament. The monarchy, the House of Lords and the Anglican Church were abolished and there was a loosely-structured national Church. The Bishops and the Prayer Book had already been abolished in 1646. Royalist, Crown and Church lands were sold to finance the conquest of Ireland (1649-1650) and crush a Scottish invasion led by Prince Charles (the future Charles II). But Cromwell's enforced union of Scotland and England did bring Scotland the advantage of free trade with a richer more prosperous country.

Cromwell won the first Dutch War (1652-1654). The English took over 1000 prizes, mostly *fluyts*, which supplied English home traders with a cheap source of cargo vessels. Oliver Cromwell's Navigation Acts of 1650 and 1651 were indirectly aimed at reducing Dutch maritime power. Cromwell allied England with

France, against Spain, and obtained Jamaica in 1665. Two more Dutch Wars followed (1665-1667; 1672-1674) and more *fluyts* were taken.

The Rump and the army commanders clashed when Cromwell, now under 'divine inspiration', tried to bring about further Puritanical changes and a 'moral regeneration' of the country. He dissolved the Rump and in 1653 ruled as a dictator (as the 'Protector') with 'major generals' acting as regional administrators and moral re-armers. There was a Royalist insurrection in 1655 which ended in complete failure. Cromwell was offered but rejected the Crown and although when he died in 1658 he was succeeded by his son, Richard, the Republic quickly collapsed. Free elections were held and within two years of his death the monarchy was restored – the people were delighted to have the monarchy back. Cromwell's body was exhumed from Westminster Abbey and hanged.

Two Rivers

In the first half of the seventeenth century the North East towns, especially Newcastle and to a lesser extent Sunderland, played important roles in the Civil Wars. Of special strategic importance were the Tyne and Wear coalfields. London was increasingly dependent on the North East for fuel and the rich pickings to be made from coal could have been an important reason for the Scots' invasion of North East England during the Bishops' War. During the First Civil War, the King's war effort was financially supported by two coal producing areas – the Tyne and Wear fields and the Severn valley.

The Crown stripped away power from the North East Earls and Prince Bishops and booming national and international trade, and lands sold to them after the Dissolution, gave more power to a developing 'commercial middle class'. Coal, especially Tyne coal, was increasingly important to the regional economy which had for so long depended on agriculture. William Gray, a Newcastle burgess and writer of the town's first history, Chorographia, in 1649 wrote: '*many thousands of people are imployed in this trade of coales; many live by working of them in pits; many live by conveying them in waggons and waines to the river Tine; many men are employed in conveying the coales in keels from stathes aboard the ships*'.

In Newcastle the Hostmen, the Lords of Coal, were the magistrates; they represented the borough in Parliament; they controlled the Tyne and its collieries; and made large capital investments in mine development and exploration on Wearside. They built the keels, which carried the coal down to waiting colliers in the Tyne and the Wear, and supplied capital to the new, booming local industries that were all heavily dependent on Tyne and Wear coal: the sea salt, the lime and the glass making industries. The region prospered. William Brereton from Cheshire visited the Tyne in 1635 and described Newcastle as '*the fairest and the richest town in England, inferior for wealth and building to no city save London and Bristow*'. Tynemouth Castle was '*a dainty-seated castle, almost compassed with the sea, wherein hath been the fairest church…but is now out of repair*'. South Shields had '*more salt works, and more salt made, than in any part of England that I know, and all the salt here is made of salt water; these pans, which are not to be numbered, placed in the river-mouth and wrought with coals brought by water from the Newcastle pits*'. The Tyne was '*plentifully supplied with salmon*' and the Quay at Newcastle the '*fairest in the land*'.

In 1637 Charles I raised Elizabeth's tax on coal (never officially a tax but a payment 'in gratitude' by the Hostmen for Elizabeth's Royal Charter) to two shillings per chaldron in a desperate attempt to make the Crown financially independent from Parliament – the opposite to what most of the country's new merchant classes, outside Newcastle, wanted. In return for the extra revenue the Crown granted the Newcastle Hostmen the right to regulate the production and fix the price of coal in the rapidly expanding industry. Not surprisingly the London importers and the East Anglian shippers (Newcastle was at first more interested in producing, rather than shipping, coal) protested and combining together they boycotted Newcastle coal in an attempt to break the cartel. Mayor Sir John Marley said '*I will not speak of what loss I sustained by the contract, but the Ipswich Puritans have so wrought the ship-men that for six weeks I did not load one chaldron of coals, so that my staithes are so full that they are likely to fire*'. The price of coal rose, the Crown's revenue dropped and Charles was forced to cancel the Newcastle cartel in 1638. The London coal importers, in the main anti-Royalist and Puritan, were given the royal right to form the Society of London

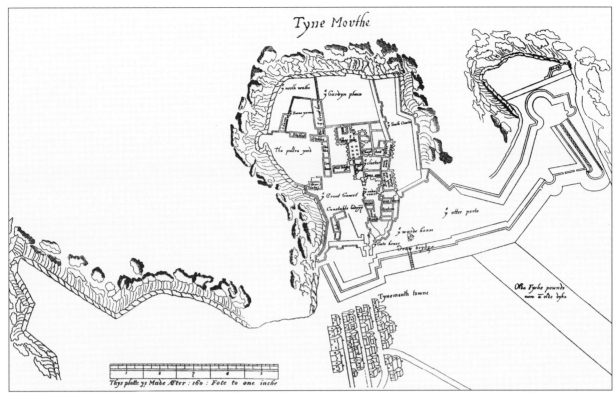

Tyne Movthe

A plan of 'Tynemouth castle', a Royalist stronghold in the First Civil War, made in Elizabeth's reign. The abbey was surrounded by a strong defensive wall and access to 'Tynemouth towne' was over a wide moat and 'draw brydge' (from the Cottonian manuscript).

Coal Merchants. The London merchants continued to boycott Tyne coal and actively encouraged the Scots to invade Newcastle and the North East coalfields. This they did in the Bishops' War of 1640 under the command of General Leslie.

The Scots occupied Newcastle in August 1640 after routing the King's forces at Newburn. The Newcastle troops, facing overwhelming odds, left the town taking their ordnance with them. There was little opposition to General Leslie, the mayor and burgesses even entertaining the officers during the first day. General Leslie was adamant that there should be no looting or stealing and all goods should be paid for. However the good relations did not last when Leslie seized Crown and Church property, confiscated mines and coal, collected customs and demanded £200 a day from the Corporation to billet his troops. Trade ground to a halt and the occupying 2,000 troops were, despite Leslie's promises, *'intolerable, insolent and voylent in their actions and discourse'*. When the General left in August 1641, complete with a Parliamentary pardon, he demanded a £40,000 loan from the town. Newcastle was later granted £60,000 by the government as compensation for the Scottish occupation.

In the First Civil War (that started a year later in 1642) Charles I, now realising the strategic importance of the Tyne and Wear coalfields, was better prepared. Coal exports could buy Dutch munitions and the Tyne would be an entry port for his military machine. Some two months before raising his standard he garrisoned Newcastle and appointed a staunch Royalist, the Earl of Newcastle, as the town governor. Sir John Marley, Newcastle's mayor and also a loyal supporter, purged the Corporation of Puritans.

In the First Civil War Newcastle and King's Lynn were the only important seaports to support the Crown. In Newcastle's case it is readily understandable. The Mayor and the town governor were Royalists. The region was both Anglican and Romanist with the majority of the people having little sympathy for what was seen as a mainly Puritan Parliament – the Puritans had only once been able to elect a town mayor and that was in 1639. The traditional enemy Scotland, although at first neutral, was strongly Presbyterian and seen to be siding with Parliament and the town was still smarting from General Leslie's humiliating occupation in the Bishops' War – an occupation that the Puritan merchants of London and the South East had welcomed as posing more problems for Charles.

Scottish troops enter Newcastle under General Leslie, 1644.

In 1640 the Council of the North was abolished and a year later the Long Parliament banned the Crown's right to collect money from any form of coal tax. In 1642 the King raised his standard and in the following year the Earl of Newcastle consolidated the King's northern position by subduing the West Riding clothing towns.

In 1642 Parliament decreed that ships were not to export coal from Blyth, Newcastle and Sunderland. In 1644, risking the wrath of the London poor (outbreaks from seamen, porters and the poor were predicted), it blockaded the Tyne coal exports *'until that Towne of Newcastle shall be freed of, and from the forces that are now raised, or maintained against Parliament'.* Annual export dropped from 145,000 tons of coal to 3,000 tons as ships visiting the Tyne dropped from some 3,000 down to 200. Coal became in short supply as London was subject to a severe winter. The London poor protested and Parliament began to lose its grip.

To ease the situation Parliament lifted its blockade on Blyth and Sunderland. This was an important moment for the development of Sunderland which had been steadily growing and developing its local salt and coal industries. Between 1609 and 1634, for example, its coal trade had quadrupled. By 1634 Sunderland was a borough with an elected mayor and, at the start of the Civil War, there were some 1400 people living in the town. Desperate for coal, Parliament encouraged Wearside mining and the shipping of coal from Sunderland to London. This was the beginning of the end of Newcastle's grip on the North East coal trade but there was not enough Wear coal to supply London. In desperation, and unable to muster a large enough army to take Newcastle, Parliament turned to Scotland for help and in 1644 formed a military alliance – the Solemn League and Covenant. It was the turning point of the war, in Parliament's favour.

In the icy winter of 1644, once again General Leslie's (now Lord Leven) troops crossed the border. But by the time he reached Newcastle the governor, the Earl of Newcastle, had departed with the town's garrison in an attempt to block the Parliamentarians progress north. Leslie entered Sunderland and then took South Shields and, with the two towns the control of the Wear and Tyne entrances. Then he too went south to link up with Parliament's forces under Fairfax and Cromwell. In a

The seal of Newcastle with its town motto 'Fortiter Defendit Triumphans' said to be given by Charles I for its gallant defence against Scottish and Parliamentary troops.

decisive battle Parliament defeated the King at Marston Moor, the result much due to the military skills of Oliver Cromwell.

Despite the victory, the London coal shortage was becoming desperate. *'Many poor have perished, being unable to buy Fewell'.* Fortress Newcastle had to fall, but the town was well fortified. Sir John Marley had deepened and lined the 'King's Dyke' with slippery clay. Outside the town walls, forts were built at Sandgate and Shieldfield; a bastion was added to the castle and a battery set up on the Quayside. General Leslie returned north and with General Callender started the siege with some 40,000 troops facing a depleted town garrison of some 1500 men. It lasted three months, but in the end mines were used to breach the town walls along with a sustained cannon bombardment from Gateshead and Castle Leazes. Marley and his men dropped back to the castle keep but they were hopelessly outnumbered and the next day he surrendered. Five days later Tynemouth castle, another Royalist stronghold, fell. John Marley was made a prisoner, but escaped to France on his way to the Tower of London to return to Newcastle after the Restoration of the Monarchy. For its courageous defence Charles I is said to have given Newcastle its town motto *'Fortiter Defendit Triumphans'.*

After the fall of Newcastle in 1644 the Scots occupied Northumberland and Durham for two years. Parliament reopened the mines of the Tyne and Wear coalfield and from taxes raised on the coal trade paid some £75,000 to the occupying Scottish army. After his second bad defeat at Naseby in the summer of 1645 Charles surrendered to the Scots who took him to Newcastle were he was lodged for nine months, apparently at Anderson Place, one of Newcastle's finest buildings. The Scottish army finally handed over Charles to Parliament for the then enormous ransom of £400,000.

The Scots left the North East in 1647. In the Second Civil War (1646-1648), Parliament took no chances with fortress Newcastle and appointed one of their loyal supporters, Sir Arthur Hazelrigg, as the town governor (he was one of the five opposition MPs Charles had tried to arrest in 1642). Hazelrigg had bought the manor and Palace of Bishops at Bishop Auckland on the Wear for only £6,000, following the 1646 Act which abolished the Durham Bishopric and put the episcopal lands and properties up for sale. (In 1648 Parliament abolished the Dean and Chapter of Durham.) As governor Hazelrigg repaired the breaches made by the Scots to Newcastle's town walls, but most of the fighting in this war was to the south and west and Newcastle, now siding with Parliament, took little part. The second war ended when the Scots, now supporting the King, were beaten at Preston in 1648.

Despite the damage and losses caused by the Civil Wars, trade on the Tyne soon picked up. The Puritans and resident Civil War neutrals,

who took over Newcastle Corporation, were just as jealous of the town's trading rights as the Royalist burgesses they replaced, continuing to keep the towns of North and South Shields in subordination to Newcastle. Ralph Gardiner of Chirton wrote *England's Grievances Discovered in Relation to the Coal Trade*

Ralph Gardiner's 1654 map of the River Tyne showing North and South 'Sheelds' harbours crammed with ships and Newcastle's quays almost deserted.

petitioned Parliament for freedom of navigation on the Tyne and the abolition of the regulations that forced traders to buy and sell at Newcastle which, he argued, caused high prices and shortages. Although Gardiner was not successful in breaking the Newcastle's burgesses hold on the river he did publish a beautiful map of the Tyne showing, in an attempt to bolster his argument, North and South 'Sheelds' harbours crammed with ships while Newcastle quays were almost deserted! The Restoration of the Monarchy in 1660 saved the Corporation from compromising its hold over the Tyne coal trade until the end of the seventeenth century.

With the peace Sunderland became an effective competitor to Newcastle as a coal producer. By 1660 Newcastle had recovered sufficiently to be exporting at its prewar levels, but Sunderland had increased production some fifty fold. Nevertheless the Tyne collieries' output was still one third greater than the Wear collieries. The Civil Wars loosened the hold of the Newcastle Hostmen on the Tyne and Wear coalfield. Soon Tyneside and Wearside entrepreneurs, often local landowners, would take over the coal production industry with the Hostmen becoming more involved in the keel traffic. The North

in 1655 where he charged Newcastle Corporation with 'tyranny and oppression'. He was imprisoned in Shields for illegal brewing in contravention of the privileges of the Newcastle's Bakers and Brewers Company. He

East glass and salt industries were quite badly hit by the Civil Wars, but there was an important development occurring in the second half of the seventeenth century: the rapid growth of North East shipbuilding.

CHAPTER NINE

RESTORATION, REVOLUTION AND REBELLION:
the birth of industry
(1658-1745)

The second half of the seventeenth century saw a flurry of activity as Continental alliances were made and broken. England ended the Second Dutch War in 1667, but within a year formed the 'Triple Alliance' with Holland and Sweden against France, then fought Holland again in the Third Dutch War (1672-1674) but 14 years later, in 1688, invited a Dutch King, William of Orange, to take the English throne. Spain's power began to wane, as did Holland's, as France became the most powerful country in the world, ruled by the absolutist, Catholic monarch Louis XIV ('le Roi Soleil', King of France 1643-1715) cousin of the English King, Charles II. By the end of the seventeenth century the powerful empire-building nations France and England were locked into a conflict that was to last, on and off, for some 150 years as they tried to gain control of the seas, ocean trade and each other's colonies.

After the death of Cromwell and the collapse of the Republic, the 'Convention Parliament', to the joy of almost all, restored Charles II (King of England, Scotland and Ireland, 1660-1685) to the throne. He had a barren marriage but many mistresses (and bastards) and presided over a licentious court. The main effect of the Republic and the Civil Wars was that the balance of power shifted away from the Crown, ruling through its councils, to the Crown ruling through Parliament. Following the 'Restoration of the Monarchy', Parliament turned the legislative clock back to those Acts that had been passed by the first session of the 'Long Parliament' and accepted by Charles I, Charles II's father (page 82). These Acts included the disbanding of many of the King's Courts and Council, the emasculation of the Privy Council and the Crown's acceptance that taxes could only be raised through Parliament. However foreign policy continued to be the domain of the King. Charles II's foreign policy lurched from one messy complication to another. In one incident he obtained money from Parliament to wage war against France while at the same time being secretly paid a retainer by the King of France, Louis XIV, whom he privately admired. In another he colluded with Catholic France against Protestant Holland in a failed and complicated attempt to bring Catholicism to Britain. But Charles II never pushed anything to the extreme, his main concern being the retention of the crown and his fear of being sent on 'his travels again'. On his death bed he acknowledged his Catholicism.

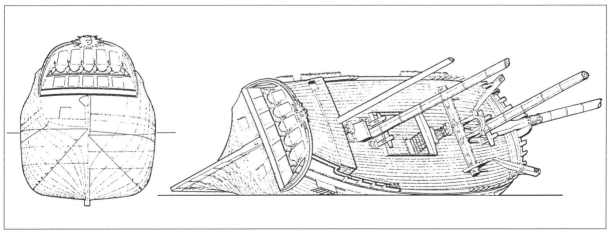

Collier 'cat barks' were U-shaped in cross section and figure heads were absent from their bows. 'Bark' (or barque) was a general name of a vessel before c. 1750 but after the term was used more specifically to describe a three masted vessel with no square sails on the third (mizzen) mast. (After Chapman.)

A mid eighteenth century model of a typical North East collier 'cat bark'. It is similar to the HM bark Endeavour *that was used by James Cook in his extensive explorations of the Pacific Ocean.* Endeavour *was 97 feet 6 inches (29.7 metres) long, with a maximum breadth of 29 feet 2 inches (8.89 metres) and the hold was 11 feet 4 inches (3.45 metres) deep.*

One of the first acts that was passed after the Restoration was the 'Act of Indemnity and Oblivion' which returned lands, confiscated by the Puritans, to the original Royalist owners. But those Royalists who had sold lands and estates to pay heavy fines imposed on them by the Puritan Parliament were not compensated. The Act was much criticised by the Royalists believing it gave 'indemnity for the King's enemies and oblivion for the King's friends'.

In 1661 a 'Cavalier Parliament' was elected which was mainly made up of Anglicans and squires. While supporting the King the Cavalier Parliament was not blindly Royalist – it kept the King short of money – as it was elected at the height of the 'Indemnity and Oblivion' controversy. But Charles, believing that it was the most loyal Parliament he could

expect, kept it in annual session for 18 years. The Parliamentary majority of Anglican squires was to be the foundation of the Tory party and its chief minister, the Earl of Danby, the party's first leader.

In 1662 the Cavalier Parliament passed the Act of Uniformity that completely restored Archbishop Laud's Anglican church and the Prayer Book (page 82). Over 2,000 Puritan clergy resigned their living as a result of the Act, which Parliament followed by the Conventicle Act and other penal statutes that persecuted Puritan non-conformists in a cruel and vindictive manner – imprisoning or transporting those caught in 'dissenting' worship. Under Charles II the jails were packed with non-conformists (Unitarians, Baptists, Presbyterians, Quakers etc) who often died in overcrowded conditions. Charles II believed that he could push Parliament to trade toleration for the Protestant Dissenters in return for toleration for his favoured Catholics. But he was wrong. The Dissenters disliked Charles and his Catholicism and the non-conformists were prepared to die for their beliefs. (They had to wait for the 'Glorious Revolution' and William of Orange before they achieved freedom of worship under the 1689 Toleration Act.)

The policies of Danby, Parliament and the 'Tory Anglican squirearchy', the landed gentry, seemed to be aimed at maintaining stability and preventing Charles II from being sent 'on tour' again. But to Shaftesbury, the leader of the opposition (mainly made up of Puritanical 'Whigs'), it appeared as if Danby and the Tories were ardent Royalists and Romanists. Charles' brother, James, had declared himself a Roman Catholic in 1670 and Shaftesbury and the Whigs desperately tried to prevent his succession. They failed as Charles' solid majority in the House of Lords voted down the 'Exclusion Bill' every time it was presented.

Towards the end of his reign Charles II had much popular support and there was a solid coalition and an agreement of purpose between the Crown and the Tory Anglican squirearchy who were responsible for the maintenance of law and order in the provinces. A trade boom was in progress and, for the first time, by Parliamentary-approved indirect taxation, the Crown had sufficient funds in the Treasury to be able to raise a standing army; an idea that would have horrified the early post Restorationist Parliamentarians. After Cromwell and the Republic, they had a fear of such armies but saw the wisdom of pouring money into Britain's effective Royal Navy to guard against foreign invasion.

When Charles II died, James II succeeded (James VII of Scotland; King of England, Scotland and Ireland, 1685-1688) and was, as the Whigs had feared, devoted to Roman Catholicism. As a result of the continued trade boom James was able to increase the size of his standing army to some 20,000 men. At first he used 'dispensing power' to appoint Roman Catholic officers (under the provision of the 'Test Acts' Roman Catholics were not allowed to hold high office and all public officers had to take Holy Communion in the Church of England) and employed raw Catholic troops from Ireland as common soldiers. But in 1687 the 'Declaration of Indulgence' was passed

which allowed Catholics to hold high office. As part of the trade, religious freedom was granted to all denominations. But the non-conformists were not fooled, seeing the Declaration of Indulgence as James' attempt to remove the Anglican stranglehold on Catholicism by creating an alliance of Protestant non-conformists and Roman Catholics against the Tory Anglican squirearchy that had control of the country.

James II married twice, the first marriage produced two daughters (who became Queens Mary and Anne) and his second marriage produced a son, James Edward Stuart, in 1688, the so-called 'old Pretender'. The Tory Anglican squirearchy (now frightened by the birth of James' son and a distinct possibility of a Roman Catholic succession) and the Whigs (the Puritan element ever consistent in their hatred of the Catholics) united and invited Dutch, Protestant William III of Orange to the country, who was the grandson of Charles I of England.

William III (or William of Orange, King of England, 1689-1702) landed in Torbay, Devon, in 1688 with an army. James II, in an emotional crisis and uncertain of his standing army, fled to France. In 1689 William (who had married James' daughter Mary in 1677) was proclaimed joint sovereign with his wife. The bloodless, 'Glorious Revolution' had taken place. William and Mary accepted the Bill of Rights, the Act of Parliament which limited the royal prerogative to ensure that the monarch ruled by law and guaranteed freedom of speech and free elections for Members of Parliament. The Bill of Rights excluded Roman Catholics from being monarchs.

William III's foreign policy was successful during his 13 year reign. He formed the 'Grand Alliance' of England, Austria, Spain and Holland that fought Louis XIV from 1689-1697. After his death, and ably led by the Duke of Marlborough, the Alliance defeated France and curbed France's continental expansionism. Mary died in 1694 and William ruled alone until 1702 when Anne, Mary's sister, succeeded. In 1707 Scotland and England were politically united, the Scottish Parliament dissolved and Scotland's executive power handed over to Westminster.

Many members of the Tory Anglican squirearchy, no longer enjoying the stability and favours they had received during the later part of Charles II's reign, were unhappy with the Glorious Revolution which they believed had favoured the Whigs. The constant continental wars had heavily and directly taxed the Tory Anglicans' estates, especially the crippling land tax. On the death of Anne in 1714 a section of the Tory party, the so-called 'Jacobites' (from 'Jacobus' the Latinised name of King James who was expelled in 1688), tried to exclude George I of Hanover (King of Great Britain and Ireland from 1714-1727) from succeeding, in favour of James II's son, the Catholic 'Old Pretender'. But the Whigs and the majority of the nation would not accept another Catholic monarch. The so-called '1715' rebellion followed, which failed and allowed the Whigs to remain in power for some 50 years. Sir Robert Walpole, as prime minister in all but name, led the government from 1721 to 1742 and, with bribery and skill, directed domestic and overseas policies that were largely based on appeasement. George II (King of Great Britain and Ireland 1727-1769) relied on Walpole for advice and during his reign the role of the constitutional monarchy was much developed.

The Second Jacobite Rebellion, 'the '45', took place during George II's reign and the Young Pretender, Charles Edward Stuart, had more success than his father. The rebellion occurred during the 'War of Austrian Succession', that lasted from 1740 to 1748. (This was a war between Austria and Prussia in which Britain at first supported Austria and France against Prussia and Spain but ended by clashing with France). Charles Stuart, or 'Bonnie Prince Charlie' as he is romantically known, landed on the Hebridean island of Eriskay with seven followers in July 1745. He crossed to the mainland and, a month later, raised his standard at Glenfinnan. Fewer clans rallied than he expected but the ones that did, the MacIntoshes, the Camerons and the MacDonalds, had an extremely successful campaign partly due to the fact that Britain was almost empty of troops. Some 5,000 Highlanders led by the Bonnie Prince easily captured Edinburgh and beat General Cope and his troops at Prestonpans with the battle lasting only minutes before Cope's troops *'ran like rabets'*. The road to England was open and the Young Pretender crossed the Border in an attempt to link up with the English Jacobites and destroy the Hanoverian succession and the Whig government before the English could raise an army. But he failed to achieve his plan (see below).

Two Rivers

The towns and villages of the Tyne and Wear were affected by and played their roles in the Restoration of the Monarchy, the Glorious Revolution and the '15 and '45 Rebellions. Following the Restoration of the Monarchy the Establishment of an increasingly commercial North East showed unusual religious tolerance, at least when compared to the rest of the country, towards the non-conformists and Catholics. The region's towns took a pragmatic view of the Catholicism of James II and the Protestantism of the Glorious Revolution which quickly followed. During the Pretender Rebellions Fortress Newcastle was, as usual, in the firing line especially in 1715 when there was a pro-Jacobite uprising in Northumberland.

After the Restoration and throughout the North East, as elsewhere in the country, Puritans and non-conformists lost their positions of power and influence. Newcastle and Sunderland Corporations were mainly composed of Anglicans and Royalists as by Act of Parliament Puritans and Dissenters were excluded from high office. Sir John Marley returned from exile (page 87) to become mayor of the Newcastle Corporation.

The Act of Uniformity (see above) resulted in voluntary resignations by the Puritan clergy (three in Newcastle) but throughout the region these dissenting ministers were not unduly harassed and most managed to make a living by either teaching or practising a profession such as medicine. A one-time Puritan minister, Ralph Ward, combined teaching 'gentlemen's sons' in Newcastle with occasional preaching, and the ex-vicar of Wooler opened South Shield's first apothecary shop. The Dissenters' practise of combining a profession with a part time pastorate lasted for the rest of the seventeenth and for all the eighteenth century.

There were a number of Scottish Presbyterians working the mines in the region and most resided at or near Newcastle. An estimate made by government not long after the Restoration of the number of dissenting congregations in Newcastle stated that there were three Presbyterian meeting houses with some 1200 members, one Unitarian with 700 members, one Independent with 100 and a small Quaker following. The Bishop of Durham, John Cosin, complained to

Newcastle's mayor that there were 'numerous conventicles held in the town' and that the town was becoming a 'nursery of faction' by allowing such 'scandalous and offensive meetings'.

John Cosin (Bishop 1660-1672) was elected to the See of Durham in 1660 following the Restoration. Bishop Cosin reintroduced Anglican worship to Wearside, endowed almshouses and restored Durham and Auckland castles. The one time Prince Bishops of Durham may have lost much as a result of the Reformation and Dissolution but they still had considerable reserves of land and wealth which were to last until the early part of the nineteenth century.

In 1674 Lord Crewe became Lord Lieutenant of the County Palatine and Bishop (1674-1721) and the County was finally enfranchised. Crewe was much liked by both Charles II and James II, and he tried but with little success to bring into effect the 1687 Declaration of Indulgence (see above). Although there were many Roman Catholics in Durham, Bishop Crewe, clearly a pragmatic man, decided to support Protestant William of Orange following the Glorious Revolution, unlike the Dean of Durham (a Romanist and supporter of James II) who fled the country.

Crewe was followed by Bishop William Talbot who, in an attempt to recover some of the Palatine's lost wealth, petitioned the House of Lords for Bishops to have the right to lease mines that were 'not accustomably letten'. The lessees of the Bishop's lands objected to Talbot's claim on the mineral rights on their leased lands and successfully fought the Bill.

Newcastle Roman Catholics, like the non-conformists, were also banned by the Act of Uniformity from building churches or chapels and held their religious meetings in private and, like the Dissenters, they suffered little religious persecution. The town burgesses were more interested in commerce than religion. (The magistrates, for example, during arch-Catholic James II reign were men of many religious persuasions: Anglican, Papist, Protestant, and non-conformist). Charles II had imposed a charter on Newcastle in an attempt to bring the town under royal control by demanding the right to appoint the mayor, sheriff, recorder and town clerk. Charles died before the charter came into effect. In 1685 James II tried to impose the royal will on the town by attempting to replace the elected members of the Newcastle Corporation with

named Catholics by a royal mandate that insisted that a 'new Common Counsell should be chosen according to custom and your charter'. The Corporation bent with the wind, sending formal congratulations to James II on the birth of his son, James Edward Stuart, but after the Glorious Revolution welcoming William of Orange. James' mandate was suspended in 1688 and in the same year the town elected a well-known dissenter, William Hutchinson, as mayor. In 1669 the local populace tore a bronze statue of James from its base in Sandhill and tossed it in the Tyne. It was later retrieved and melted down for a set of bells for All Saints church – a bronze leg was donated to St Andrews!

The towns of the Tyne and Wear were anti-Roman Catholic following the Glorious Revolution in 1689. There was a scare in Newcastle in 1696 when a French invasion in support of James II was anticipated off Tynemouth but it came to nothing as did a Jacobite rebellion in 1708 in Scotland. The Northumbrian Tory gentry believed that a Jacobite Restoration was the only way in which they would recover their finances – many of their estates were almost ruined by the land tax that was used to raise money for the wars. In 1715 when the Earl of Mar raised 'James III's' standard on the Braes of Mar north of the Border, the Catholic Highland clans and Scottish Border lords gathered and declared their support. In Northumberland, at Rothbury, seventy five local gentry with their retainers joined the Earl of Derwentwater, the son of one of Charles II's bastard daughters, and declared their allegiance to the Old Pretender. Thomas Forster, an Anglican Tory MP, was made General with the hope that the rebellion would have a wider appeal than just to Roman Catholics. He led the march on Newcastle.

But Newcastle was ready and waiting. All potential Jacobite supporters in the town were arrested and some 700 extra recruits enrolled in the local militia. The tough keelmen even offered to stand to arms. The rebels hesitated and it was long enough for a considerable body of dragoons, led by General Carpenter, to arrive on the Tyne. Carpenter marched his troops north and the Northumbrian Catholics retreated into Scotland where they linked up with the Earl of Mar's forces. The rebel army split with one section marching south. Fortress Newcastle blocked the route east so the rebels travelled south and west via Carlisle to capture Preston. General Carpenter approached the rebels from the rear, marching south west from Newcastle, while troops led by General Willis came north from Wigan to attack the rebels' front. Outmanoeuvred and outnumbered, the rebels surrendered. On the same day the Duke of Argyle defeated the remainder of the Earl of Mar's forces at Sheriffmuir. When the Old Pretender landed at Peterhead, some five weeks after Sheriffmuir, the rebellion was already over. Forster escaped but the Earl of Derwentwater was executed, some 30

Bucks' view of Newcastle (engraved between 1727 and 1753). Three masted vessels alongside the quay, single masted coasting vessel and sailing and rowing, coal-carrying keels above and below the bridge.

English rebels were hanged as an example and many of the Scottish prisoners, taken at the battle of Sheriffmuir, were transported to the American colonies. The old Northumbrian Catholic country gentry suffered much as their estates were seized and sold and not surprisingly the new gentry gave the next Jacobite rebellion little support.

The 1745 rebellion, for the Young Pretender, was better led and had more support north of the Border than the 1715. Six weeks after his win at Prestonpans (see above) Bonnie Prince Charlie came south. Once again Newcastle was well prepared: all suspected Jacobites had been arrested, 800 extra volunteers were enrolled in the town militia, the town walls were repaired and strengthened, all but three wall gates were blocked up and some 200 cannon were deployed on the ramparts and towers. The 1745 was taken seriously by the government and some 20,000 regulars under General Wade arrived and were billeted on the Town Moor.

With Newcastle blocking his way Bonnie Prince Charlie had no option but to invade England via the west coast route. Carlisle surrendered and the rebel Prince continued south. General Wade left Newcastle only to return when he realised that the quickly-moving Highland troops were far to the south

of him. The Duke of Cumberland, the youngest son of George II, was in command of the main British force. Cumberland came north and ordered Wade to join the pursuit of the Highlanders who were, by then, returning northwards in some disarray after reaching Derby. But Cumberland was forced to return south to deal with an expected French invasion and Bonnie Prince Charlie rounded on the pursuing English forces, led by General Hawley, and defeated them at the battle of Falkirk. But it was a short-lived victory. Cumberland returned north and on his way to Scotland passed through Durham and Newcastle. In Durham the mayor and Corporation welcomed him – the local MP even presented him with a horse. In Newcastle his presence unleashed a number of unpleasant incidents against local Catholics and their places of worship. Cumberland decimated the Highlanders in 1746 at Culloden Moor near Inverness and became known as the 'butcher' for his troops bayonetting of wounded Highlanders where they lay. For his victory he was given the freedom of Newcastle, and its inhabitants celebrated with a display of fireworks followed by all-night drinking and dancing in the streets. Culloden Moor was the last battle fought on British soil.

After the Civil Wars and despite the disruptions of the Jacobite Rebellions, the Restoration and the Glorious Revolution, North East industry prospered. Small factories and workshops abounded and Newcastle, North Shields and Sunderland were overhung with palls of smoke that on a clear day could be seen from the Cheviots. London by 1650 was totally dependent on Tyne and Wear coal and colliers not only carried the coal but were a major part of the British Merchant Navy. The colliers of the North East coal trade supplied many seamen for the Royal Navies of Charles II and James II: as early as 1615 it was noted that *'The Newcastle voyage, if not the only, yet is the especial nursery and school of seamen'.*

Mighty Newcastle on the Tyne and fledgling Sunderland on the Wear clashed. As far back as 1660 the Newcastle Hostmen had claimed their charter rights (page 74) in a bid to control the growth of Sunderland and the Wear coal trade by imposing a one shilling tax on all coals exported from Sunderland. The Hostmen were acutely aware of the threat the rich coal seams of the tidal Wear below Chester-le-Street posed to their monopoly of the coal trade. Their monopoly was finally broken when from 1700 to 1750 the volume of coal production nearly doubled (national production rose from 2.25 million tons to more than 4.75 million tons) and non Hostmen Tyneside and Wearside entrepreneurs became involved in the rapidly expanding coal business. Even by 1700 Sunderland was shipping more coal overseas than Newcastle although Newcastle still had the grip on the British coastal trade.

In 1710 the North East pit owners, ever keen to form monopolies, formed a consortium of coal producers, 'The Regulation', to control coal output, production and shipping to their captive market, London. By 1700 London accounted for some 80% of Newcastle's coal trade and the Regulation could prevent the loading of a Tyne collier if the consortium considered that the vessel had already exceeded its monthly London shipping quota. As the coal trade increased so did the number of co-partnerships; one of the most famous was the 'Grand Allies' made up of the Ravensworth, Strathmore and Wortley families. These coal-producing consortia fought local landowners who tried to charge excessive rents for the miles of wagon ways that were increasingly being laid to carry coal from pit head to staithes.

At first the Newcastle Hostmen rarely owned the colliers that shipped their coal, although they often had shares in them. In the seventeenth century most colliers were built and owned by East Anglians; towards the end of the century they were built and owned by Londoners but this had changed again by the 1750s when the major shipowners and builders resided in North East ports – Newcastle, Whitby, Scarborough and Sunderland. Daniel Defoe wrote of Newcastle in 1727 that: *'they build ships here to perfection, as to strength and firmness and to bear the sea, as the coal trade requires.'*

By the early 1700s the average collier carried around 240 tons of coal, nearly a four-fold increase since the 1600s. The Dutch fluyt prizes obtained from the Dutch wars were gradually wearing out and, as the eighteenth century evolved, the North East shipbuilding ports developed the 'cat bark' or 'collier cats'. These vessels had a three masted rig of the 'bark' type with the aft-most mast (the missen) carrying a triangular fore and aft sail and the first two masts (the fore and main) carrying square sails. These North East 'cat barks' (probably named after the similar but earlier Dutch vessel whose name was derived from the Scandinavian 'Katschips') had sturdily built hulls that were less pear-shaped, with broader stems and sterns, than the Dutch fluyts in order to maximise their cargo carrying capacity. Their nearly flat bottoms allowed them to sit upright and be worked at low tide on exposed beaches. The famous Captain James Cook, Pacific navigator and explorer, served his apprenticeship in the North East coal trade and chose a 'cat bark' for his famous South Sea voyages (pages 90 & 91). (A career as a merchant ship's officer was often followed by the sons of the local, minor, landed gentry.) The more efficient, two-masted collier 'brig' replaced the three-masted cats by the end of the eighteenth century (page 98). These seaworthy 'Geordie brigs', typically 200 ton vessels each with a crew of some ten men, increasingly made trips to London in the winter time. By the 1750s most ships built on the Tyne were colliers with only the occasional warship. The largest ship then built on the Tyne, launched by the Headlam yard, was the collier *Russell*, capable of carrying 30 keels of coal.

John Forster, who lived in 1648 on Low Street, Sunderland's main street, is one of

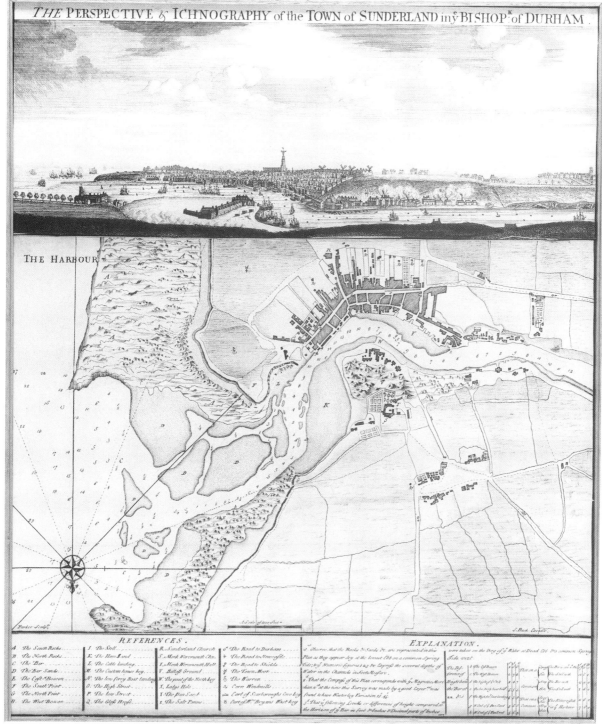

Buck's view of the entrance to the River Wear which looks south across the river towards Sunderland and was probably drawn c1720 before work started on the piers. St Peter's church is shown on the north bank and there are glass works and salt pans on the south bank at Bishopwearmouth Panns. Just visible to the right of the Panns is Bishopwearmouth's St Michael's church. The spire of Holy Trinity church dominates the centre of Sunderland.

Wearside's first recorded shipwrights. In 1672 records first refer to the Goodchild family, shipbuilders on the Wear for the next 150 years, who constructed 80-90 ton ships for transporting lime from their lime kilns at Pallion. In 1705 a petition to make the Wear a more navigable river was sponsored by the Durham Guilds of Mercers, Grocers,

Haberdashers and Salters who hoped to make the river passable to Durham. The Newcastle Corporation, jealous of the Wearsiders, tried to stop the Bill. A Newcastle resident stated that the Wear's *'bar is so choaked up that there is a great want of water… If any storm arises at sea there is no safety in offering to go into Sunderland'*. However the bar at the Tyne entrance was not much

An early nineteenth century two masted collier brig (from E.W. Cooke, 1828, Shipping and Craft*).*

better. In 1717 the Wear Improvement Bill was passed and the River Wear Commission created. Owing to the rocky nature of the river bottom it proved too difficult a task for the Commissioners to make the Wear navigable as far as Durham and in 1795 their jurisdiction was cut back to Biddick Ford. The Commissioner's income was a biannual tax on coal exports and by 1730 there were sufficient funds to construct a South Pier to improve the rate of water flow and deepen the harbour entrance by forcing a water stream through the bar. The river was dredged in 1749 and the north channel blocked by sunken barges to improve water flow though the south channel. The River Wear Commission regulated the keelmen and fined both colliers and keelmen for dumping ballast into the river, a perennial problem in the Tyne. In 1765 the Tyne had *'so deteriorated through neglect and the dropping overboard of ballast that where ships used to load and lie afloat at low water was dry in several places'* (Hodgson). It was not until after 1850 that the Tyne was deepened by its Improvement Commission.

By the middle of the seventeenth century there were many local records to testify to the rapid growth of the riverside industries of the Tyne and the Wear. Alum refined for dyes, especially in Sunderland; there were brewing, brick making, lime making for fertiliser, smelting of lead, copper brass and tin, and sea

salt and glass-making. In 1682 Ambrose Crowley started an iron works on the Wear at Sunderland with skilled French workers and, eight years later, he built another works at Swalwell on the River Derwent, a tributary of the Tyne navigable up to Swalwell, for the production of heavy forgings such as cannon carriages. He also founded a works at Winlaton for the production of lighter metals such as cutlery and hand tools. At first iron was smelted using charcoal but it was not long before the coke-using blast furnaces were employed in the production process.

By the early 1700s coal had replaced charcoal as the fuel for many British industries and all the Tyne and Wear riverside industries were dependent on a plentiful and cheap supply of coal. By 1700 the salt industries of South Shields and Sunderland were booming with the coal mines of the Tyne and the Wear supplying some 70,000 tons of coal for their salt pans each year.

The early part of the eighteenth century saw major advances in coal mining technology. On the Wear at Chatershaugh Colliery a machine using water as a counter weight and a steam engine was successfully used for the first time to haul coal out of a pit, a job previously carried out by horses. Everywhere there were improvements in shaft and tunnelling technology. Deeper pits in the Tyne and Wear coalfield were also made possible with the introduction of Newcomen's steam pumping engines which pumped out water and vastly improved the drainage of the mines. But with deeper pits came the increased risk of methane explosions. In 1705 an explosion killed 30 Gateshead miners and in 1708, at Fatfield near Chester-le-Street, 69 were killed. By 1700 wagon ways with wooden rails were not only being used to connect the pits with the riverside staithes but rails were also being laid in underground galleries.

The Civil War had been less kind to Newcastle's glass industry than to South Shields' and Sunderland's, which were growing rapidly and were soon, especially Sunderland, to compete with Newcastle. At one time Newcastle had a monopoly of the British glass industry which may have started as early as

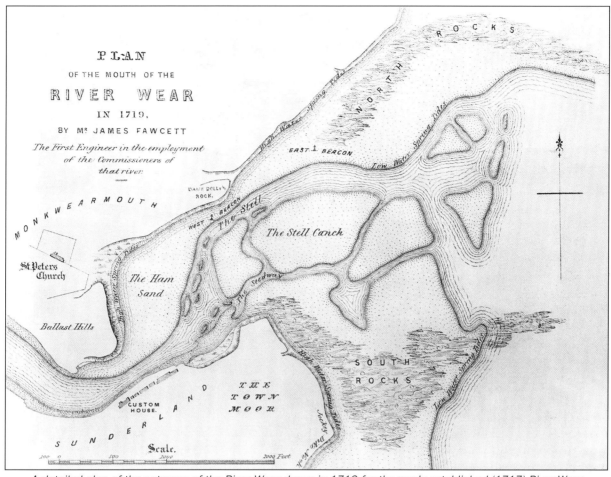

A detailed plan of the entrance of the River Wear drawn in 1719 for the newly established (1717) River Wear Commissioners. Coal, lime, salt and glass were the major exports from the Wear but the river was shallow and choked with dumped ballast and sandbanks.

1577 when a Newcastle Alderman is recorded as having obtained drinking glasses from a local glasshouse. In 1615 King James II banned the use of wood for glass making in order to conserve timber supplies for the Royal Navy. Sir Robert Mansell, a favourite of James, was charged with developing a technique to make glass from coal. He was successful at Newcastle where *'after the expense of many thousands of pounds, that worke for window-glasse was effected with Newcastle Cole'*. Mansell set up three furnaces at Newcastle and invited skilled Protestant glass-workers, religious refugees from Lorraine, to work his furnaces. In 1640, at the time of the Scottish occupation of Newcastle, Mansell had 1,200 cases of glass windows ready for shipment to the south. By 1696 there were 11 glass furnaces and the glass makers used sand in the construction process that was collier ballast. Carefully crated glassware was shipped out of Newcastle on top of the coal in the ships' holds and the colliers

sailed back to Newcastle, in ballast, their holds filled with sand. The Newcastle glass makers became especially skilled and developed some delicate glassware, notably the Light Baluster, in response to the Glass Excise Act which taxed glass by weight and was responsible for the collapse of a number of English glasshouses. In 1737 there were two glass houses on the South banks of the Tyne and glass was being produced at works on the quayside in South Shields. The Sunderland Company of Glassmakers was established in the 1690s and by 1772 Sunderland had four quayside glass works. It was soon to become world famous for its glass industry.

With the exception of heavy engineering, all the Tyne and Wear riverside industries that the region was to become nationally and internationally famous for, were in place by 1745. The Industrial Revolution, fuelled by the coal mines of the Tyne and Wear coalfield, was now quietly underway. Soon it was to explode.

CHAPTER TEN

COMMERCE, INDUSTRY AND STRIFE:
cotton, coal, ships and steam
(1745-1815)

The eighteenth century was a remarkable century for England and led to the development of 'Britain' as a superpower. The first British Empire might be considered to date from 1763, the end of the Seven Years' War, when Britain had the best of the struggle against its main empire-building rival, France. The Anglo-Dutch conflict ended when William became King in 1689 but his succession to the throne was one of the causes of the many English-French conflicts. There were five great wars during the eighteenth century: the Spanish Succession 1702-1713; the Austrian Succession 1739-1748; the Seven Years' War 1756-1763; the War of American Independence 1776-1783 and the Napoleonic Wars 1793-1815. Only in the American War of Independence was Britain on the defensive and, as a rule, after each conflict England gained more overseas possessions from the nations which formed an alliance with France. After losing the Battle of Trafalgar in 1805 France was never again such a powerful maritime nation. The Battle of Waterloo in 1815 sealed her fate on land.

Throughout the eighteenth century Cromwell's Navigation Acts were in force which were designed to increase Britain's share of world trade whereby imports to England could only be carried by English ships or in ships of the country of origin. After the Act of Union in 1707 Scottish ships had access to English trade and colonies and the Act of Union was to lead to Britain becoming the maritime superpower and adopting the title 'Great Britain'.

George III (King of Great Britain and Ireland, 1760-1820, and grandson of George II), unlike the previous two Kings who had strong roots in Hanover, never visited Hanover. In his first address to Parliament, he stated that *'Born and educated in this country I glory in the name of Briton'*. He was keen to govern as well as reign but much-blamed, along with Prime

Minister Lord North (through whom George III exerted Parliamentary influence by maintaining North's parliamentary majority with royal patronage), for the loss of the American colonies. He called Pitt the Younger to office in 1783 but by 1810 George III was permanently insane.

The growth of English shipping in the eighteenth century was phenomenal, increasing from 340,000 tons in 1686 to over a million tons in 1788. The European nations fought one another throughout the 1700s for control of the oceans and commerce but Britain had the merchant ships, the Royal Navy and above all the will to fight: *'It was a foolish game; but while everybody played it, those prospered most who could play it best. Every war left Holland, whether our (England's) enemy or our ally, a little more exhausted. Every war administered a check to French commerce. Every peace treaty added to the markets open only to British traders and the ports only open to British ships. Canada and Newfoundland became British. The British East India Company found in the rapid growth of their possessions and spheres of influence in India more than sufficient compensation for their exclusion from the Malay Archipelago (by Holland)'* (Ernest Fayle.)

Whig and (during the second half of the century) Tory Governments aggressively pursued Britain's commercial interests. Pitt the Elder, leader of the 'Patriot Whigs', became Secretary of State in 1756 (although he was effectively Prime Minister) and had particular success in the Seven Years War (1756-1763). In the East, powerful trading companies with Government support conquered lands and people. In India, inevitably, the French and English East India Companies clashed. In 1751 Robert Clive of the East India Company took Arcot in 1751 and in 1757 re-captured Calcutta from the French. In 1763 the British overran the French trading post at Pondicherry and by 1769 the French East Company was dissolved. The Seven Years War was a clear struggle

The East Indiaman the Earl Balcarras *built in 1815 and considered one of the finest examples of an Indiaman ever built for the English East India Company.*

between France and England; fighting was mostly at sea with Britain usually the victor. Britain decisively beat France in India and Canada and Britain's other gains included Florida, part of Cuba and Manila in the Philippines. By the Treaty of Paris in 1763 Britain was a world super power. The only setback during the 1700s was the loss of the American colonies and their important supplies of cheap timber for Britain's ever expanding mercantile fleet. Over a thousand trees were required to build a ship such as the *Earl Balcarras* (a large Indiaman) for the English East India Company.

The American colonies revolted against the British Government's authoritative rule and its attempt to tax the colonies without their representation. France, Spain and Holland joined with the thirteen colonies to blockade and oppose Britain and Britain lost. The success of the 'American Revolution' probably created the political climate that was to lead to the decline of the monarchy in the western world. The war was not as popular in Britain as were other eighteenth century wars. In Newcastle, for example, the local populace usually reacted to the news of the outbreak of yet another war with spontaneous street demonstrations and jingoistic 'huzzas', but not so with the news of the American War. Members of the Newcastle Corporation even expressed their dissatisfaction with the declaration of war by a letter to Government. After the war, however, Anglo-American trade continued, with Britain exporting manufactured goods and exchanging slaves and gold from the African Gold Coast, in either the Caribbean or America for sugar, tobacco, tar and timber – the 'slave triangle' first set up in Elizabethan times.

One of the most important reasons for the Industrial Revolution was that the colonies gave Britain's manufacturers a vast, ready-made, export market for manufactured goods, especially cotton: the colonies were not only there to be exploited or act as dumping grounds for Britain's dissident and 'criminal' population. After the French revolution in 1789 Napoleon Bonaparte once again turned Europe into a battlefield and war continued at sea. But after winning the Battle of Trafalgar Britain's position as mistress of the sea was secure for over 100 years. The Royal Navy closed Britain's colonies to any other country, yet Britain was powerful enough to force other countries to open up their ports to British goods! It was policy that made Britain the 'workshop of the world' and served the country well until the end of the nineteenth century.

Although in 1750 agriculture was the most important element of the British economy from then on, and until the early twentieth century, overseas trade and manufacturing were to develop into the twin peaks of the British economy. Manufacturing developed from overseas trade and led to the Industrial Revolution which started, almost imperceptibly, from around 1750. Industrialisation happened gradually and its roots lay in the opening up of the oceans to trade that had occurred in the two preceding centuries. At first overseas trade was the more lucrative part of the economy and by 1745 British ships were sailing east and west round the globe protected by the most powerful of Britain's weapons – the Royal Navy. But it was the manufacturers, the industrialists, especially the textile-makers, who increasingly had a say in government policy. By the end of the eighteenth century more British people were involved in the manufacturing process than were in trade. British kings (unlike Continental kings) were subordinate to Parliament and, although Parliament was still controlled by the landowning upper classes (Parliamentary seats from the estates and rural towns still

outweighed those of the developing industrial towns and ports), Parliament tended to be on the side of the merchants who made up the core of commercial England – the middle classes – which was not only composed of rich merchants but also successful, entrepreneurial craftsmen and small tradesmen. By 1800 England was indeed a 'nation of shopkeepers', a phrase first used by the Scottish economist Adam Smith (1723-1790) but normally attributed to Napoleon Bonaparte.

The towns grew rapidly throughout the second half of the eighteenth century, especially the western sea ports of Glasgow, Liverpool and Bristol as they traded in slaves and colonial goods. London had over a million inhabitants and was by far the largest town in Europe. The first Official Census in 1801 of England, Wales, Scotland and Ireland revealed that the population stood at 15.74 million, a rise of some 25% from the estimated population of around 12 million in 1750. Some 30% of the people in mainland Britain lived in towns, many of them small rural market towns but a significant proportion of the population lived in the western seaports.

Manufacturing gradually increased its share of the gross national income from about one fifth at the beginning of the eighteenth century to a quarter by the end of the century and just outstripped the proportion of the national income from trade. There was a decline in the importance of land and the agricultural industry in the British economy fell from an estimated half of the total national income at the turn of the century down to about a third by 1800. By the end of the eighteenth century agriculture was being treated as a commercial asset and developed and exploited in much the same way as industrial enterprises. Food was not imported in bulk until the middle of the nineteenth century; until then British farmers had to feed the British people.

Throughout the 1700s, the enclosures continued converting uncultivated, often 'common land', into enclosed fields mainly in the Midlands and sometimes at the expense of the rural poor and subsistence cottager. Throughout Britain land was owned by the large estates which rented it out in parcels to tenant farmers who cultivated it through hired labourers. Farms gradually grew larger and farming methods more efficient but the rural poor had less land for themselves and depended more on selling their labour for wages. By the end of the eighteenth century the Industrial Revolution was not sufficiently advanced to absorb the excess rural labour force that was the result of the agricultural changes and a rapidly-expanding population. Bad harvests and economic slumps caused riots and urban unrest. The Poor Laws (which from the sixteenth century made the birth-place parishes of the poor responsible for looking after the poor) were often used to send 'foreign poor' back to their parishes, particularly in the south and east where there was little developing industry to help improve conditions. There was no national police force and in the fast-growing industrial towns mob riots were common (especially after bad harvests) and the local militia were often called out to restore order, sometimes with loss of life. The forces available to the state to control a discontented population were limited but the Penal Code was used as a deterrent. It was harsh and arbitrary; men could be hung for sheep stealing, pick-pocketing or other relatively minor offences as well as murder. Public executions were common.

From the middle of the eighteenth century there were marked improvements in domestic communications especially with the development of the nation-wide turnpike system. Turnpike Trusts were set up from about 1730 to 1770 and were responsible for the injection of capital into the development of the roads especially in the North. Canals were dug and they were a very efficient means for the transport of bulk freight. The dramatic improvement of the transport system infrastructure opened up the domestic markets to the products of the Industrial Revolution – in the second half of the century the domestic market grew by some 40%. But the export market grew by a staggering 200% with textiles being the major export, representing some 60% of the total exports by 1800.

For the middle class entrepreneurs of eighteenth century Britain, especially those living in Manchester and in Lancashire, enormous profits could be made relatively easily from the machine production of cotton. The steam engines of the Industrial Revolution were fuelled by coal and coal output doubled during the second half of the eighteenth century. Iron was increasingly in demand for armaments, bridges, machinery and machine parts for the new cotton mills. Late eighteenth century advances in iron production technology, where the ore was smelted with coal and the metal 'puddled' and 'rolled' to produce wrought iron, resulted in a doubling in iron production during the last twenty years of the century such that by 1800 Britain was an exporter of iron.

Eighteenth century Britain was increasingly plutocratic with the Elizabethan grammar

The Wallsend Colliery that reached the deep Main Seam.

schools often nurturing the future officer classes and middle class business men. Admiral Lord Collingwood, for example, second in command to Nelson at the Battle of Trafalgar, was born in Newcastle in 1750 and educated at Newcastle's Royal Grammar School. It was Britain's growing band of reasonably-well-educated, urban middle classes, together with the skilled metal workers and crafts people that supplied the new, applied technology that placed industrialised Britain ahead of a non–industrialised world. The explosive power of the nineteenth century Industrial Revolution was a gradual speeding-up and development of the inventions and processes that had already occurred in the eighteenth and earlier centuries. Britain became the nineteenth century world super-power and the North East played a vital role.

Two Rivers

The number of coalmines along the banks of the Tyne and Wear approached its peak towards the end of the eighteenth century. On the Tyne, pits were opened up to the east of Newcastle to reach rich, but deep (over 700ft), seams: Willington, Felling, Walker, Wallsend, Jarrow, Percy Main and South Shields. They were closer to the sea which meant that the owners were less dependent on the keels and 'rebellious' keelmen as colliers could more easily come alongside to load coal from the staithes. By 1800 Britain was producing 10 million tons of coal a year. London consumed two million tons a year, over nine tenths of it supplied from the Tyne and Wear coalfield. By the end of the eighteenth century it was estimated that some 75,000 people from the Tyne and Wear earned a living from the coal industry.

But life was hard for the coal miners and their sons. Conditions underground were appalling with foul air, underground floodings, roof collapses and methane explosions being everyday risks. Young boys worked ten hours a day down the pits once it was realised that seven and eight year olds could control the pit ponies while older boys worked even longer hours, performing boring, repetitive tasks. The miners, often lying on their backs and 'hand-hewing' coal with pickaxes from 20 cm high seams, would return exhausted to the surface after eight or ten hours of intense manual

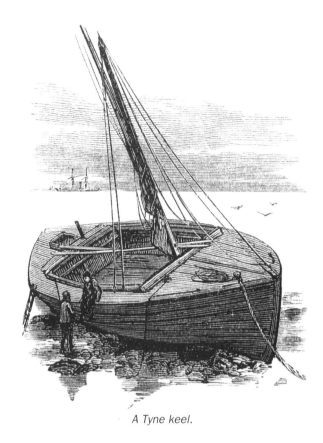

A Tyne keel.

labour. Tsar Nicholas I of Russia, on viewing the main shaft of a Wallsend pit, commented that: *'It is the mouth of hell; none but a madman would venture into it'.*

Coal mining was a seasonal trade (as was the keelmen's) before the development of the all-weather, steam-powered collier in the nineteenth century, although, as wooden ship design improved, colliers were increasingly making winter trips to London. Such was the demand for coal that by 1770 20% of the total amount of North East coal was exported to London in winter and colliers were making about six trips a year. Miners worked for a yearly bond and were paid a yearly 'binding fee' of sixpence or a shilling by the colliery owners. At first this bonding worked well to both employers' and employees' advantage until the end of the Seven Years War when there was a trade boom, an increase in demand for coal, and a shortage of miners. Employers were forced to offer higher binding-fees, sometimes as much as three guineas. To reduce costs owners collectively agreed that they would only employ a miner if he could produce a certificate of discharge from his previous employer. Owing to the labour shortage no employer would issue such a certificate, thereby binding miners to employers for life. The owner's bonds were often harsh (miners were jailed if they violated them) and miners were paid according to volume and not weight of coal they produced. There were severe financial penalties for short measures, stone-contaminated coal, or even coal that was not of the correct size and it was possible for a miner to owe the owner money after working a shift! Bonds also forced miners to shop in the company store for their picks, clothing and low quality food. In 1765, not surprisingly, most of the miners in the North East coalfield, some 4,000 men, went on strike. The coal trade was brought to a standstill for several weeks until the owners conceded the pitmen's right to change employers when their yearly bond expired, but the owners refused the miners' request for better wages and conditions. In 1789 the miners struck and rioted and this time their wages were raised, but the yearly bond still remained in place.

There were improvements in mining technology. Thomas Newcomen's steam engine had solved some of the problems of underground flooding and by the late eighteenth century foul air was removed from the mine by a two shaft system whereby an 'upcast shaft' pulled bad air out of the mine with a small furnace and men and ponies went down the pit by the 'downcast' shaft. Although the double shaft system was effective at improving underground air quality many colliery owners refused to install it because of the extra costs involved. Some pits were immensely profitable to the owners but profits were not generally passed on to the miners. Inventions like the Davy and Stephenson Safety Lamps did much to reduce the risk of underground explosion from methane gas but often just resulted in the owners sinking deeper, more difficult shafts. Nevertheless by the end of the eighteenth century there were improvements in pay and conditions and by then the North East miners were some of the highest paid workers in Britain.

The other body of labourers associated with the coal mining industry on the Tyne and Wear were the keelmen and, like the pitmen, they were bound for a year with their binding day traditionally Christmas Day. In 1700 there were 1,600 keelmen working the Tyne from some 400 keels, double-ended lighters with a single square sail and a large sweep oar for steering, that were typically crewed by a

A coal staith that brought about the demise of the Tyne and Wear keels and keelmen.

Late eighteenth century engraving of the Port of Tyne with Clifford's Fort and the leading lights into the Tyne.

skipper, two crew and a boy. The keelmen became an independent society in 1556 but they never became an incorporated company because the Hostmen, the Newcastle burgesses and their paymasters, were concerned that they would lose their hegemony. The paternalistic Newcastle Hostmen clashed with the keelmen as they tried to control the Keelman's Hospital which was built in 1701, by the keelmen themselves. The bishop of Ely is said to have said that he had seen and heard of '*many hospitals, the work of rich men; but that it was the first he ever saw or heard of which had been built by the poor*'.

The Tyne keelmen lived in Sandgate and Henry Bourne, the Newcastle historian who wrote a town history in 1736, described the region as a vast number of narrow lanes crowded with houses. John Wesley disapprovingly described the inhabitants of Sandgate thus: '*much drunkenness, cursing, and swearing even from the mouths of little children, do I never remember to have seen or heard before in so short a space of time*'. The keelmen rioted and went on strikes, particularly in 1709, 1710, 1740 and 1750 which were more about lack of food than pay and conditions. In 1740 after a particularly severe winter and bad harvest they joined up with Newcastle pitmen and local

poor and in one incident they attacked the town court, destroyed records and went off with a sum of money. A rioter was killed and the Alnwick militia had to be called to disperse the mob. In 1761 some 5,000 went on the rampage throughout Northumberland and it took two battalions of the Yorkshire militia to stop them.

In 1794 the Tyne keelmen struck again, this time over the use of staithes for loading the colliers: they were right in believing that direct loading of the colliers would soon destroy their livelihood. As the eighteenth century progressed, coal was increasingly carried to the river in horse-drawn wagons running on wooden then iron rails which led to staithes where the colliers were berthed. At first the coal was dropped into the colliers' holds through 'spouts'; later, in order to reduce breakage, the coal was loaded with 'coal-drops'. The Tyne spouts were first introduced around 1750 but not until about 1812 on the Wear. There were about a thousand keelmen working the Wear in 1800 and they rioted in 1815 when coal was moved by the first wagonway to the spouts. But change was inevitable and by the middle of the nineteenth century coal was increasingly transported by railways to the colliers moored at the Tyne and

Wear staithes. The centuries-old keelman's trade was finished. They were a hard working, tough breed and Sunderland born Jack Crawford, a national hero, was a Wearside keelman. In a hail of musket fire he re-hoisted the colours of the Admiral's flagship, the *Venerable*, by nailing them to a broken mast during the height of the bloody Battle of Camperdown that was fought between the English and Dutch in 1797. Crawford became the symbol of the bravery of the ordinary seaman.

Away from industrial Tyneside and Wearside most of the settlements along the upper valleys of the two rivers and the Border region were, in 1750, poor and backward with much of the land being forest or barren fell. Much of the region's richest land belonged to the Bishop of Durham and by the early part of the eighteenth century was already 90% enclosed. In 1773 there were at least 600,000 acres of unenclosed common in Northumberland and that *'from the north point of Derbyshire to the extremity of Northumberland, of 150 miles as the crow flies, which shall be entirely across waste lands'*. The main crops were oats and rye and the industrial regions on the banks of the Tyne and the Wear were dependent on the southern, eastern regions for wheat. As the century progressed large stretches of the 'waste lands' were enclosed with little opposition from the local populace. By 1810 over a quarter a million of acres were enclosed in Northumberland and Durham and there were vast improvements in agriculture. Crop rotation, drilling, turnips for winter feeding (before winter feeding with turnips most sheep and cattle were slaughtered and salted for winter food), new threshing machines, improved stock breeding methods all resulted in improved yields and productivity. Daniel Defoe wrote in *A Northern Tour:* '*A few years ago little was to be seen but barren wastes; now, large tracts of country are enclosed, farm houses built, and the land so well cultivated so as to produce very good corn and grass'*.

There was industry even in the countryside. The 'Lead Dales', the valleys of the East and West Allens and the South Tyne, the Derwent and Upper Weardale had produced lead since the time of the Romans. After the Norman conquest the Bishops of Durham owned many

of the lead mines and made money by both leasing and claiming royalties on the lead. The orefield was so rich that by the seventeenth and eighteenth centuries Britain was the world's largest producer of lead, and during the eighteenth and nineteenth century most of the population of the Lead Dales depended on lead mining. In 1809 there were four mines in the Derwent valley and 34 in Weardale and £5,000 of royalties were paid to the Bishop of Durham. Lead production peaked in the mid-nineteenth century but the lives of the lead miners in the remote and wind-swept villages of the upper reaches of the Tyne and Wear were as bad, if not worse, than those of the coal miners who worked the pits nearer the sea. At first the lead ingots were carried by pack horses over the moors along the 'leadways' to the staithes on the Tyne and Wear. Later valley

Wearmouth Bridge. When it was built in 1796 it was considered to be one of the industrial wonders of the world.

roads and the Alston turnpike were constructed but it was the coming of the railways in the middle of the nineteenth century that made the industry boom before it rapidly declined in the 1870s as a result of overseas competition.

Before the railways, turnpike roads played a key role in improving communications and opening up the domestic market. In 1751 a turnpike road was built between Newcastle and Carlisle and it is still known as the 'west turnpike' or 'military road'. By 1815 turnpike roads connected Durham, Sunderland and Newcastle and a west bound road ran along the Wear valley up to Alston. A post road ran from London to Berwick, via Durham and Newcastle, and there were regular weekly mail coaches.

Newcastle's medieval bridge was built in 1250 and repaired after a flood in 1339. The central section was destroyed by a flood in 1771.

The other important eighteenth century transport system – the canal – made little impact on the North East, probably because river and sea transport was so well established and some saw the coming of the railways. The Tyne was, according to Lord Mulgrave, capable of becoming one of the finest rivers in the world. But, still controlled by the monopolistic Newcastle burgesses and suffering from the conflicting commercial interests along its banks, the river was fast becoming a shallow,

'cursed horse-pond' as the returning colliers continued to dump ballast into the river and the bar at the river mouth continued to be a source of danger to shipping. Gardiner's map (page 88) clearly shows the dangerous bar.

The Wear, however, was gradually being improved by the River Wear Commission. In 1771 the Wear flooded and destroyed the foundations of the South pier (page 111). But by 1785 the Commission had re-built an improved South pier and by 1795 constructed

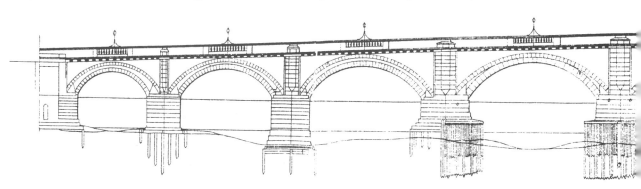

The Newcastle stone bridge that was built between 1773 and 1781 to replace the medieval bridge.

a 700 foot long North pier. An octagonal lighthouse was built on the end of the North pier in 1804 and with the improved facilities coal exports from the Wear continued to rise. In 1790 Sunderland was exporting three quarters of a million tons a year compared to Newcastle's one million tons.

There were some improvements on the Tyne. Two new 'leading lights' to help ships enter the Tyne were built by Trinity House at North Shields in 1805, to replace the lights that were built in 1727 but were made redundant when the river changed its course. The river pilots pushed for greater safety measures on the Tyne and in general they were sorely needed on both the Tyne and the Wear. Thousands of ships cleared the port of Sunderland and left the Tyne each year. In one period in 1800, out of 71 colliers that headed to London from Shields and Sunderland, only three survived the trip. In 1789 the Newcastle-owned collier brig *Adventure* went ashore on Herd sands and locals watched as the ship was pounded to pieces by the waves – only five of the thirteen-man crew survived. Horrified, the leaders of the South Shields shipping community commissioned Henry Greathead to produce a boat that could be launched into large waves for the purpose of saving lives. Greathead built 35 'lifeboats' between 1798 and 1810 and they were a great success – his first lifeboat, supported by the Tyne Lifeboat Institution, was to save 200 lives in eight years. The Wear followed suit and soon the 'Sunderland Committee' had their own lifeboat and in 1811 fitted their boat with airtight compartments to increase buoyancy.

Outside the North East the cotton industry was driving the Industrial Revolution but on the Tyne and Wear it was coal, lime, glass, lead and iron production that were the major industries of the late eighteenth century. Glass

and iron production were already established in the region by 1750 and both industries rapidly increased during the second half of the century with the number of glass houses on Tyneside increasing from sixteen in 1772 to thirty by 1812.

Great improvements in iron production technology, such as Darby's method of smelting iron ore with coal rather than charcoal and Watt's rotary steam engine in 1782 to drive the bellows and work the huge hammers of the forges, enabled the North East iron producers to meet the increasing demand for iron: iron for the coal industry, shipbuilding, armaments, engines, bridges (the iron bridge over the Wear was built in 1796 by Walker's of Rotherham) and soon the railways. The wooden rails for horse drawn trucks above and below ground in the coal industry were gradually replaced by iron rails, the first in 1797 by Thomas Barnes who ran them from his Walker pit down to the Tyne. The first cast iron rails were brittle and prone to snap. New malleable iron rails were more successful but not laid in the North East until 1820 when the Bedlington Iron Works started to produce them in quantity. In 1814 the first North East steam boat was launched, the Newcastle-North Shields ferry the *Perseverance*, the small beginning of the North East's world famous iron and steel shipbuilding and heavy engineering industries.

Of great importance in 1802 was the invention of the high pressure steam engine – the puffer – by the Cornish mining engineer Richard Trevethick who visited Newcastle in 1804. It soon became apparent that 'travelling steam engines' could pull wagons of coal along the wagonways more efficiently than horses. In 1813 Christopher Blackett, the owner of the Wylam Colliery on the River Tyne, commissioned the famous *Puffing Billy* to haul coal from Wylam to Lemington. George

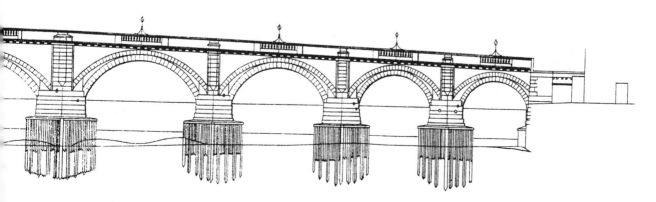

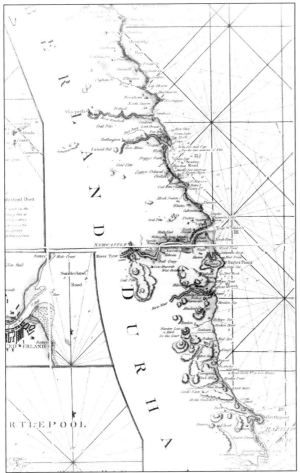

A coasting chart published in 1794 by Laurie and Whittle, London. The inset shows the entrance to Sunderland.

Stephenson, engineer at High Pit, Killingworth, designed his locomotive in 1814 for Lord Ravensworth's collier railway – it was the true fore-runner of the railway locomotive.

In keeping with the rest of Britain, there were rapid increases in the population of the North East from the middle of the eighteenth century. In 1750 Newcastle's town walls were still intact and there was one bridge across the river that had stood since the fourteenth century. Newcastle historian Henry Bourne described how most of the town's 20,000 inhabitants lived down by the river although there was some migration of the wealthy away from the quayside area. As the population increased the town began to overflow. The new Tyne bridge, with nine arches and made of stone, was built in 1781 but because of increased traffic it had to be widened in 1801. When Britain's first official Census was conducted in the same year, Newcastle's population had risen to 28,294. In comparison, Gateshead's population was 8,597 and South Shields with Harton and other surrounding villages was 12,909. On the Wear Sunderland

had a population of 12,412 but the three combined settlements at the entrance to the Wear – Monkwearmouth on the north bank, Bishopwearmouth on the south bank and adjacent Sunderland – was 24,000, almost equivalent to Newcastle. John Rain, parish surveyor, left a superbly detailed, if not superbly drawn, map of Sunderland and Bishopwearmouth. It was completed between 1785 and 1790 and shows the range of industries present on the banks of the Wear.

By 1815 the lower reaches of the Tyne and the Wear were well industrialised. On the Wear lime production was one of its most important early industries along with coal, glass and chemical works. To be found on one or both river banks were coke and tar factories, potteries, paper mills, rope works, iron foundries, chemical and glass works, breweries, lead works and shipyards. The Tyne and Wear sea salt industry was in decline following the extraction of cheaper rock salt from Cheshire but the chemical industries were on the rise as alkali, for example, was needed in large quantities for the local glass and Lancashire textile industries. But all these industries came at an ecological price. The Tyne and Wear were on their way to becoming seriously polluted rivers and salmon returning to the upper reaches to breed, once abundant and a source of food and income, were soon to return no more.

There were shipyards at North and South Shields, Newcastle and Sunderland. The Newcastle Guild of Shipwrights had been granted Guild status in 1604 and they had the exclusive rights for building and ship-repair on the Tyne. On the Wear, although the staple trade was exporting coal (and lime), rapid advances were occurring in the shipbuilding industry. There were six working yards in Sunderland in the 1780s and by 1790, 2,736 tons of wooden shipping were produced. In 1805, as a result of the increase in demand from the Napoleonic Wars and the loss of the American colonies (which had supplied much of Britain's merchant fleet prior to the War of Independence), the Sunderland shipyards produced 14,198 tons of shipping. Newcastle's tonnage exceeded Sunderland's in 1805 but, in an industry that was always subject to cyclical fluctuations, in 1814 Sunderland produced 14,000 tons, probably exceeding Newcastle's. Sunderland was about to became the greatest shipbuilding port in the world.

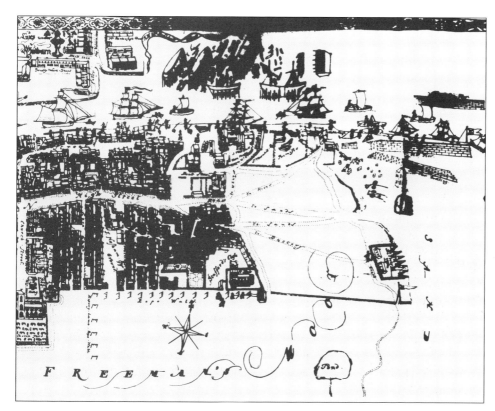

Rain's Eye Plan of the River Wear c1785. The plan shows shipbuilding on the north bank, coal-carrying keels and two masted ships being towed up and down the river by oar-powered 'foys'. The Wear's North Pier was under construction and was built between 1786 and 1797. Building started on the South Pier in 1723 and continued for many years. In 1750 the north channel, the Stell, was blocked and the south channel, the Sledway, opened (Fawcett's 1719 map, page 99).

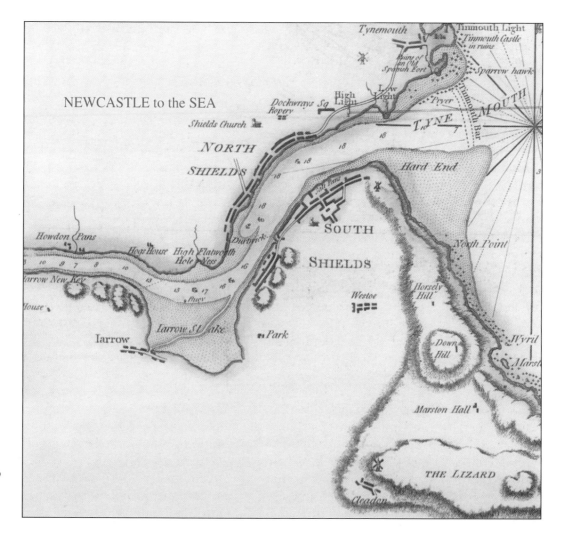

The Tyne entrance according to Laurie and Whittle 1794.

CHAPTER ELEVEN

THE GLORY DAYS: radicals and railways
(1815-1914)

The nineteenth century was Britain's century. Britain became the world's richest super-power, the pioneer of industrial economics, the trail-blazer of international capitalism and throughout the century Britain's power and expansionism were unstoppable. The technology, the expanding population, the Merchant and Royal Navies and the desire to create international markets enabled Britain to take the Industrial Revolution to the world. By the 1860s the British Empire was the largest empire that the world had ever seen.

Britain became the world's first urban nation as its countrymen flocked from the land to the new industrial towns. Overseas, as a general rule, the British flag followed British trade in the continued empire-building process when powerful chartered companies, like the East India Company, collapsed or were taken over by the British government. Britain was strategically positioned in the North Atlantic, had numbers of well-protected harbours, enormous reserves of coal and low-grade iron-ore and a skilled workforce. Britain made the ships and the goods the rest of the world wanted and was indeed the 'workshop of the world'. During the Napoleonic Wars, when smuggling was rife and the Royal Navy effectively blockaded the French ports, the British textile industry even clothed Napoleon's armies.

For the first half of the century textiles, especially cotton, were the driving force of the economy. From 1850, just when it looked as if the Industrial Revolution might falter, coal, iron, steam engines, ships, steel and especially the railways dominated the economy. From about 1830 there was a glut of capital as the booming textile industry created unprecedented wealth and within two decades over £240 million was invested in trains and track as 'railway fever' gripped investors. Although the railways were not always a good investment, the laying of thousands of miles of track did much to drive the second phase of

the Industrial Revolution. Many men were employed in the construction process and a superb transport infrastructure, roads, canals and the railways, did much to create a *national* British economy.

George IV (King 1820-1830) became regent in 1811 after his father George III was declared insane. In 1820, the year of his succession, he unsuccessfully tried to divorce Queen Caroline whom he had agreed to marry after secretly and illegally marrying a Roman Catholic widow. George IV's gluttony and dissolute behaviour put the monarchy in disrepute and it was not restored when he was succeeded by eccentric and outspoken William IV (King 1830-1837). William had a barren marriage, despite having ten children by his actress mistress, and was succeeded by his niece, the dignified Queen Victoria (Queen 1837-1901). She did much to restore the crown's prestige during her long reign and, during the latter part, the public identified her with the nation's achievements.

But Britain's achievements did not come easily. In the first half of Victoria's reign there was hardship and poverty in the countryside and the booming industrial towns as Britain entered the unchartered waters of the Industrial Age. Philosophical radicalism, often promoted and led by artisans, the new skilled labourers and the middle class 'radicals', resulted in demonstrations by the working classes in the towns and the countryside against the unemployment, overcrowding and poor work conditions that the industrialisation process was producing. At first the workers lacked the vote but the tremendous increase in the nation's prosperity and the radical movement brought about dramatic changes during Victoria's reign to enfranchise and 'liberate' the working classes. By the end of Victoria's reign modern constitutional government was born.

At the end of the Napoleonic Wars in 1815 unemployable soldiers and sailors returned home and many industrial workers were left without work as Britain switched from a war to a peace economy. A severe slump gripped the country: half a million hand loom weavers starved as the new machines took over production and war-torn Continental Europe could not afford the price of British goods. When the price of wheat fell in 1815 many farmers were ruined overnight. Cottage industries declined as the new factories took over their work. The powerful, landed interest pushed Parliament to pass the Corn Laws in 1815 which prevented the import of wheat until the price of home-grown wheat had risen to a certain level. The aim was to guarantee farmers' (and land-owners) incomes but disastrous harvests in 1815 and 1816 drove up the price of bread. Bread was the workers' staple diet and on average they each consumed around 340 gm (c. ¾lb) each day.

In the beginning of the nineteenth century workers' dissent was more often about food than emancipation and the right to vote. The Tory, mildly reactionary, Liverpool administration (1812-27) was attacked by the Whig opposition who skilfully used the rapidly expanding local media – pamphlets and regional newspapers – to whip up popular support. But in 1819 in Manchester the 'Peterloo massacre' did much to enrage the radicals and politically active working class. When some 50,000 people gathered to hear radicals demand universal suffrage the local magistrates panicked and ordered the speakers arrested. Eleven people died in the press and ensuing panic after a body of hussars arrived.

The new coal driven, smoky factories of the Industrial Revolution were employing women and children in preference to men. Parliament outlawed trade unions and since the workers did not have the right to vote, there was much industrial unrest. In response the government suspended Habeas Corpus in 1817 and Acts were passed which took away some of the workers' liberties, including their right to hold public meetings. Riot and industrial sabotage became more common place, the Tower of London and the Bank of England were attacked and extreme radicals even plotted to assassinate the Cabinet.

In the early 1820s the grain harvests improved and there were changes in the Tory government that were more sympathetic to the 'working classes'. The Corn Laws were eased and anti trade union legislation repealed along with the restrictions on workers' freedom. The

Navigation Acts (pages 83, 100) were also repealed and the criminal code overhauled and made less severe.

In 1830 Earl Grey became the Whig Prime Minister and formed a government that promised peace and reform following an election that was precipitated by the death of George IV. Although the Whigs advocated more liberal parliamentary reforms they were against a secret ballot and votes for the working class. The opposition Tories were led by the Duke of Wellington. In 1831 the winter was again harsh and the reform agitation, often led by middle class industrialists or professionals who believed that workers should have the vote, reached near revolutionary pitch. Grey resigned when, for the third time, his Reform Bill was mauled by the Lords. Wellington and the Tories, sensing serious countrywide unrest, dropped their opposition to the Bill.

The Reform Act was passed by the Lords in 1832. Although hailed as a triumph for liberal parliamentary reform it only increased the size of the middle class vote. The average size of the English electoral boroughs, which returned the 658 Members of Parliament, was less than 900. In Newcastle, for example, before the Reform Act, 3,000 freemen out of a total population of 53,000 had the vote; after the Act this number was only increased to 5,000. However the 1832 Act did reduce corruption and the selling of votes. It was followed in 1833 by legislation that regulated children's factory hours and slavery was finally banned throughout the British Empire. In 1834 the Poor Law Amendment Act was passed. Up to then funds for the poor had come from parish property rates, but as the rates and the population grew there was a demand for a change in the law. With the Amendment Act poor relief was less readily available and those seeking help had to enter the prison-like conditions of the workhouse. Families were forcibly broken up. A Poor Law Commission was set up and 'poverty' became legally defined. The Poor Law System stayed in place until 1947. The Mines Act of 1842 forbade the employment of women and girls underground in mines, as well as boys under the age of ten.

The British aristocracy were little affected by the Industrial Revolution; if anything they gained from increased rents and the extraction of minerals from their lands. The rich middle

British steamships, often built on the Tyne and Wear and fuelled by North East coal, challenged and then gradually replaced sailing vessels on all the ocean trading routes.

and business classes were keen to join the privileged lives of the upper classes and there was a continued fusion of the well-off in land, industry and commerce. As the mid-Victorian period approached British society became more complex, more varied and more mobile. The labouring classes were confronted by the ostentatiously wealthy and flamboyant, often garishly built, municipal buildings and the richly furnished houses and magnificent country estates of the new middle, entrepreneurial and upper classes. It was not surprising that the aims of Chartism – the ballot, votes for all men, equal electoral districts, MPs to be paid and not needing to own property to be elected, annual Parliaments – appealed to many of the working classes.

The Chartist Movement was most active from 1838 to 1842 as depression struck the British economy and once again the harvests were very poor. It was not surprising that Chartism was considered to be highly dangerous and threatening to the landed oligarchy; the near-revolutionary situation of the 'hungry 1840s' between the working and ruling classes was only saved by the economic boom of 1843. As renewed capital investment drove the economy and, as a result, unemployment rapidly dropped, the appeal of Chartism faded. Britain now entered an economic golden age. Coal and iron production, steamships and especially the railways – from 1830 to 1850 some 6,000 miles of track were laid in the United Kingdom – drove the second phase of the Industrial Revolution. By 1840 British-built steamships were challenging sail on the ocean trading routes.

In 1846 the radical 'Anti-Corn Law Leaguers' continued to criticise the Corn Laws as intended to protect the Tory, land-owning elite at the expense of the consumer. The Law was amended in 1828 when a sliding scale was introduced. Sir Robert Peel reduced the duties in 1842. They were abolished in 1846 to allow the free importation of corn and from 1850 onwards Britain prospered mightily. By 1851, for the first time in British history, more people lived in the towns than in the country. For the next 20 years the mid-Victorian industrialists and traders promoted the 'Liberal State': egalitarian capitalism with the emphasis on self-reliance and self-help. 'Free trade', the removal of all tariffs, was the country's main economic philosophy with 'free trade' being the synonym for unbridled Victorian entrepeneurism and empire-building that took place in a time of economic boom. The Great Exhibition of 1851, organised by the aristocracy, showed Britain as the manufacturer of the world and the free-trade movement went hand in hand with the new economic growth. Palmerston, a Tory who joined the Whigs in 1830, became Prime Minister in 1855 to head a Liberal coalition and actively pursue the shambles of the Crimean War (1854-56), when large numbers of troops were moved for the first time by sea. He was known as 'Firebrand Palmerston' and, according to the historian H. C. Matthew: *'personified the bombastic self-confidence of Britain as the only world power, and succeeded in being simultaneously an aristocrat, a reformer, a free-trader, an internationalist and a chauvinist'.*

British technology, heavy engineering and manufactured goods were exported to the world. The colonies were the primary source of raw materials and were, as was the rest of the world, the market for Britain's manufactured goods. Countries reluctant to trade were often forced to: Chinese markets were opened up by British warships and Japanese by American warships. London became a centre of finance, specialising in shipping, insurance, the investing of British money overseas and the source of capital for the new industrialising countries. By the end of the nineteenth century Britain's industrial might was on the decline, challenged by America and Germany. Although by 1914 heavy engineering employed more workers than any other sector, Britain never recovered from the First World War and the loss of competitiveness.

In 1832 a Cholera epidemic swept through Britain, killing over 30,000 people. In an attempt to improve the country's health, water closets were introduced although at first they often drained into the poor's drinking water! By 1854 Medial Officers of Health were compulsorily appointed to the cities and responsible for sewage, clean drinking water and general slum clearances. The working week with non-working weekends began to appear around 1850, as did a provincial and national Liberal press. (The Liberal 'Party' was a loose middle/upper class coalition with its main ideology being a commitment to free-trade.) In 1850 an Act was passed that resulted in the appointment of Government Inspectors of Mines and by 1867 factory legislation was passed to improve workers' conditions. Parliament passed acts in 1871 and 1875 that improved further the rights of trade unionists. Real wages doubled between 1860 and 1914 and the powerful, rich, well-established industrialists were now sufficiently confident to accept that there was little chance of them becoming bankrupted by the workers! During the second half of the nineteenth century, politics was dominated by Prime Ministers Gladstone and Disraeli. Gladstone, initially a Tory, became Liberal Prime Minister and led the Liberals for four parliamentary terms (1868-1874, 1880-1885, 1886, 1892-1894).

The 1867 Reform Act was very much the work of Disraeli. It gave more working class males a right to vote and allowed the Tories, led by Disraeli (Prime Minister 1868, 1874-1880), a chance to be reelected in 1868. The Liberals under Gladstone passed the Education Act in 1870 and the Ballot Act which introduced secret ballots. As a rule the Tories under Disraeli did not reverse Liberal legislation. The Tories created County Councils and their 1902 Education Act was the fore-runner of secondary education.

In the countryside during the last fifty years of the nineteenth century there was a rapid decline of the agricultural economy (and continued rural depopulation) which fell from some 20% of the national income down to some 6%. British farmers no longer fed the British people and most of the island's food was imported. Religion played little part in the lives of the industrial workers but seaside resorts boomed and national holidays, railway trips, rambling, betting on horses and football clubs all became part of the British workers' way of life. The middle classes bought up land for recreation.

When Queen Victoria died in 1901 Britain had a huge overseas Empire but at home industrial capitalism was producing poverty and it was finally recognised that Victorian *laissez-faire* had created many disadvantaged poor. By 1911 there were over 40 million people living on mainland Britain, 80% were urbanised as rapid industrialisation and population growth caused the towns and villages close to the earliest industrial cities to merge to produce vast urban 'conurbations'. From 1850 to 1911 cities like London doubled their population (2.3 million to 4.5 million) and almost quadrupled if Greater London was included. By 1911 there were over three quarters of a million people living on Tyneside as the riverbank towns merged. For the first time the government recognised poverty as a social phenomenon and legislated against it. The modern welfare state was introduced by Liberal governments (1905-1914) which passed legislation creating old age pensions, national insurance, free school meals and labour exchanges. The Labour Party was created in 1906 (renamed from the Labour Representation Committee that was formed in 1900) and, representing the working classes, was increasingly associated with the trade union movement which grew from a membership of some two million in 1901 to four million by 1913. The Labour Party had a great boost when in 1909 the coal miners switched their allegiance from the Liberal Party to Labour.

Although Britain ruled the waves, when Victoria's son Edward VII became King (1901-1910) the Royal Navy had little influence on the affairs of Continental Europe and those events that led up to the First World War. When George V (King 1910-1936) came to the throne, Britain's land forces were depleted and most of the country's military expenditure went towards building up a fleet of *Dreadnought* battleships. Germany, united after the Franco-Prussian War (1870-1871), replaced a politically divided France as Britain's traditional enemy. Germany rapidly industrialised to become one of Europe's most powerful nations and the country had sufficient reserves of iron and coal to be independent of Britain. The Imperial German Navy was rapidly expanded and when ten German liner companies, representing some 60% of German shipping, amalgamated, British merchant shipping had a serious competitor for the first time in nearly 100 years. Germany began collecting colonies and, inevitably, clashed with the greatest coloniser since the Romans. The Boer Wars (1880-1881 and 1899-1902) had fuelled the rivalry between the two nations and when, in 1914, the German army marched into Belgium the traditional British concern over the strategic importance of the Low Countries was threatened. The British Empire reluctantly went to war. World peace, so vital to free trade, and the glory-days of Pax Victoriana were over.

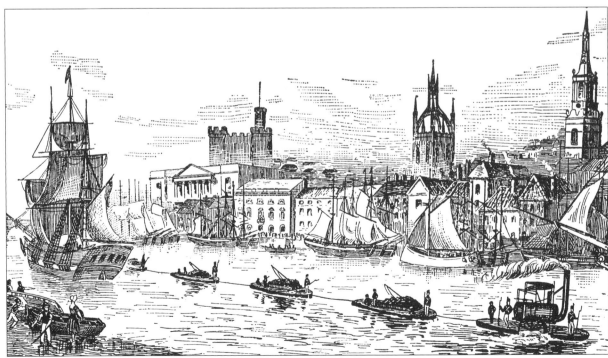

The attempt to break the 1822 Keelmen's strike on the Tyne.

Two Rivers

The end of the Napoleonic Wars caused at least as much, if not more, hardship in the North East than in the rest of the country. The return of the soldiers and sailors (nearly half of British seamen were from the North) along with the fall in demand for armaments, ships and war materials, meant that miners, shipbuilders, factory and iron workers were laid off and regional unemployment soared. The high price of bread drove the unemployed workers to civic violence and the liberal middle classes supported them by drawing up anti-Corn Law petitions (some 25,000 people signed the 1815 Newcastle petition). For weeks on end unemployed sailors prevented ships from sailing out of the Tyne and the Wear as they tried to force employment out of the local shipowners. In Sunderland in 1816 the poor looted and burnt provision ships and the local food market was raided and over-run by a mob. In North Shields in 1819 marines opened fire on rioting seamen and keelmen. In 1822 the Tyne and Wear keelmen went on strike and, fearful for the loss of their jobs, physically attacked the recently-constructed coal loading staithes where colliers loaded coal directly from wagonways that connected to the pithead. On the Tyne a locomotive was placed on a keel and the 'tug' used to tow the keels in an attempt to break the strike. The strike lasted ten weeks before it finally collapsed.

Radicalism was embraced by the North East intellectuals and artisans and reform societies abounded, notably the Political Protestants of Newcastle and Neighbourhood. Throughout the region pamphleteers and the local liberal press raised 'workers' awareness' and generally drummed up support for the radical movement. The Political Protestants organised a meeting on Newcastle's Town Moor in 1819 to remonstrate against the Peterloo Massacre (see above). Some sources estimate that 20,000 people, along with representatives of all the local reform societies, took part in the demonstration. The meeting went remarkably peacefully even though Lord Durham had to stand up in Parliament and deny a rumour that 15,000 armed men from the Tyne and the Wear were about to start a rebellion! However the Newcastle burgesses took no chances and, after the demonstration, raised extra troops and swore in additional special constables.

The North East miners attempted to raise support for a trade union in 1831 by holding open meetings at Black Fell near Chester-le-Street and on Newcastle Town Moor. The miners went on a ten week strike for better working conditions and they were able to obtain some concessions from the owners, notably limiting the working day to 12 hours for boys. The employers tried to prevent the spread of trade unionism and in 1832, with the aid of soldiers and special constables, broke up a violent, four-month-long strike during which a policeman and a miner were shot and a magistrate was murdered. In 1841 the Miners Association of Great Britain and Northern Ireland was formed and in 1844 the Association supported a strike by the Tyne and Wear pitmen against the bonding system (page 105). After five months the owners broke the strike by bringing in outside labour and evicting local miners from their homes, but this time the strike did help to end the bonding system which was more or less disbanded on Tyneside, although it survived on Wearside for some 30 more years.

There were workers' demonstrations in many of the towns on the banks of the Tyne and the Wear in support of the 1832 Reform Bill. The local aristocracy, the Duke of Northumberland and the Bishop of Durham and other local peers, had all voted against the Bill in the House of Lords and, as a result, there was much resentment from the North East's radical middle and working classes. But near revolution turned into widespread celebrations when Wellington, the Tories and the House of Lords were finally forced to drop their opposition to the Bill. But the Reform Act did little to enfranchise the region's workers even though four new constituencies were created: Sunderland with two members; Gateshead, South Shields and Tynemouth each with one member. The representation of the rural areas of Northumberland and County Durham was raised from four to eight members while Newcastle and Durham remained unchanged with two members. Since there was such a small increase in the number of people allowed to vote it was surprising that Lord Grey was so popular with the northern people. On his return to his family seat at Howick Hall in Northumberland in 1832 he was given an enthusiastic reception in all the local towns through which he passed. Newcastle Corporation even named Newcastle's finest street after him and built an

Contemporary drawing of evictions that took place during the 1844 miner's strike.

impressive 'Grey's monument' to celebrate his parliamentary reforms.

Chartist fervour spread violently throughout the North during the late 1830s and early 40s. There were reports of armed gangs of workers roaming the region and mobs went on the rampage in many of the towns. However, the repeal of the Corn Laws, improving harvests, an expanding economy, the rapid growth of the railways, falling unemployment and a more liberal parliamentary regime did much to alleviate the unrest. As coal exports, iron railways and steamship construction boomed in the North East the working class forgot about the vote.

The intensive nineteenth century industrialisation of the Tyne and the Wear occurred mainly in the eastern part of the region with the population increases associated with the Industrial Revolution occurring largely in the towns on the banks of the lower reaches of the two rivers. There was a proliferation in the number of pit villages of the Northumberland and Durham coalfields and one-industry towns, like Consett which depended on iron, sprung up almost overnight. Tynedale and Weardale, however, were relatively unaffected and some of the market towns even shrank in size as the

inhabitants moved down to the factories and shipyards of Newcastle and Sunderland. Durham, once such an important town in the evolution of the region, played little part in the process of industrial expansion.

Newcastle grew from a population of 87,784 in 1851 to 271,523 in 1914. On the Wear in 1801 there was a total of 24,000 inhabitants living in three separate settlements: Monkwearmouth on the north bank and two separate ones on the south bank. One settlement was on land 'sundered' from the monastery, Sunderland, and the other was Bishopwearmouth. By 1914 the combined population of the three settlements (unified as a County Borough) was 150,000.

Since the Middle Ages the people in the towns of the North East were used to the sight of raw sewage running down channels cut into the middle of narrow streets and seeing it piled alongside the roads in 'middens'. But in the nineteenth century overcrowding made the situation far worse. Because of the general lack of public transport nineteenth century industrial workers were crammed into hovels near their workplaces and the everyday smells in the slum areas of Newcastle and Sunderland must have been terrible. Dozens of families were served by a single water pump and people

International boat race on the Tyne at Newcastle, July 1866.

late to save the centuries-old, Tyneside, salmon-fishing industry: decades of serious organic pollution were beginning to act as a barrier to any salmon returning to breed. In 1912 a water sample taken at Newcastle Quay recorded zero oxygen content and soon the Tyne was to be devoid of fish.

Despite ever increasing river pollution, throughout the nineteenth century the Tyne and the Wear played important roles in the region's leisure activities. The Tyne, before the river became too polluted, was England's finest salmon angling river and skiff racing on both rivers was an important recreational activity both as a participatory and a spectator sport. Tyneside oarsmen like Clasper, Chambers and Renforth were not only local heroes but household names throughout Britain and the rest of the boat-racing world. On race days over two hundred thousand people would line the banks of the Tyne to watch them drive their beautiful lightweight skiffs through the water. Harry Clasper, born in 1812, was a Tyne keelman who became the undisputed British rowing champion. His successors were equally successful: Bob Chambers became the World Champion, and James Renforth, rowing for Britain,

rarely washed after working long hours in the factories and mines. In 1842 a report on Gateshead housing complained that: *'each small, ill-ventilated apartment of the house contained a family with lodgers in numbers from seven to nine, and seldom more than two beds for the whole. The want of convenient offices induces the lazy inmates to make use of chamber utensils…which remains in the most offensive state for several days and are then emptied out of the window.'* (Chadwick Report, 1842).

By 1850 both raw sewage and industrial waste were being poured untreated into the rivers in unprecedented amounts. The deepening of the Tyne and the Wear for the increased river traffic was to have unforeseen adverse effects on the cleansing action of the tides. It was estimated that raw Tyne sewage lingered for up to ten days in the river and was pushed upstream by the incoming tides to settle on the river bed. Only towards the end of the nineteenth century was government legislation passed to improve health and reduce water pollution: in 1875 the Public Health Act and in 1876 the Rivers Pollution Prevention Act. By then it was too

James Renforth dying in the arms of friend and fellow crewman Henry Kelley.

dramatically died during an epic race for the World Championship in Canada in 1871. Both men worked in Tyneside factories or foundries and both died young – Chambers at the age of 37 and Renforth at 29 – and their sport died with them. In the 1890s association football became the region's most popular spectator sport, as it is today. Once a year on Ascension Day the mayor of Newcastle, the Corporation and the members of Trinity House marked their long-held jurisdiction over the Tyne with a ceremonious river parade of gaily-decorated barges. It ended when Newcastle's control of the river was lost to the Tyne Commission in 1850, although the parade did take place once every five years until it was finally abandoned in 1901. On the Wear rowing was an important component of the Wear Regatta which was held annually from 1834 until 1914.

The boom in the railways and steamships that took place around the mid-nineteenth century created a massive increase in demand for North East iron for manufacturing and coal as a source of power. Ironworks were built at Consett (Consett Iron Works), Bishop Auckland (Witton Park Ironworks) and at Stanhope and Tow Law (Weardale Iron and Coal Company). The richest iron deposits in Britain were being mined at Eston in Cleveland by 1850. As the century progressed the iron industry moved from the Tyne and the Wear further south to the River Tees as Middlesbrough and Darlington became major iron-producing centres. Cheap steel production was introduced in the 1870s by the invention of the Bessemer and Siemens forging process. In the 1880s the Consett Iron Company switched over to steel production but the steel industry, like the iron industry it replaced, continued to be centred around the Tees.

To meet the ever-increasing demand for fuel new coal mines were sunk in the Tyne and Wear coalfield at Gosforth, Wideopen and South Hetton near Houghton-le-Spring (in 1822 George Stephenson constructed a railway connecting this mine with the port of Sunderland). Other mines were sunk between the city of Durham and the east coast, at Seaton, Murton, Trimdon, Castle Eden and Shotton. A 1,700ft deep mine shaft, the deepest shaft in Britain, was sunk with much difficulty at Monkwearmouth. Pit villages sprang up as some 500 pits were sunk in the County of Durham. The government in the general spirit of free trade repealed all coal

taxes and, more sensibly, nineteenth century coal was sold by weight rather than by 'chaldrons' or 'keels'.

The unceasing demand for coal, the power source for the national economy, meant that pits were dug deeper and, coupled with the use of explosives, it was almost inevitable that serious accidents occurred. In 1835, for example, 102 men were killed following an explosion in the Wallsend pit and in Stanley in 1909 168 men died. After failing in their protracted 1844 strike (see above) the Northumbrian miners finally formed a union in 1872. The Durham miners were still bonded to the owners up to 1872 but their Association, formed in 1869, managed to break the bondage system and the Durham miners soon had the largest union in Britain. The Durham Miners' Gala was started in 1871.

The keelmen had, by riot and strike, managed to prevent the building of staithes on the lower reaches of the Tyne until 1820. Previously, in 1815, when coal was moved by wagonway from pits to the staithes built above the Wear bridge, Newcastle troops and cavalry were called out to restore order as rioting Wear keelmen tried to break up the staithes. The 1822 keelmen's strike (see above) where there were violent clashes between the keelmen and the authorities is seen as a milestone in the history of labour. One of the reasons that the coal-exporting Seaham Harbour was built five miles south of Sunderland by the Marquis of Londonderry was to bypass the militant Wear keelmen. Londonderry custom-built a railway-fed harbour and the first coal from Londonderry's Rainton mine left Seaham Harbour in 1831. Seaham Dock and Harbour were enlarged in 1845 and an overflow railway line built to connect with the Port of Sunderland staithes.

At the staithes coal wagons were placed in cradles and bodily lowered down to the colliers which were moored alongside the staithes. Coal dropped out of bottom doors in the wagon directly in to the ships' holds. Later coal was loaded directly from wagons that were discharged into one of a number of different 'chutes', each with a different outlet or 'spout' so that loading could take place at any state of the tide. As the railway network grew, coal loading staithes were built at North and South Shields, at Hay Hole, Wallsend and Pelaw on the Tyne and on the Wear at Newbottle and Hetton. By 1830 over 50% of the coal exported

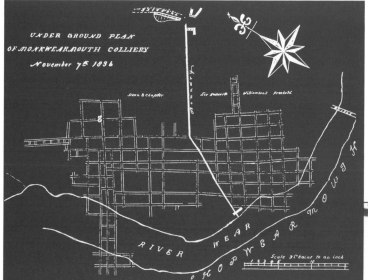

Above: Underground plan of Monkwearmouth Colliery.

Right: 'Sinkers' during the excavation of the Monkwearmouth Colliery in 1864.

Below: 'Drops', which lowered coal wagons to the collier's deck, and 'chutes' at the Wallsend staithes which signalled the demise of the Tyne and Wear keelmen. (T.H.Hair, 1844).

The original staithes, South Dock, River Wear. The coal wagons were lowered down to the collier's deck and the coal had less far to fall to enter the ship's holds.

A collier brig unloading coal. (E.W. Cooke, 1828).

Plate 6. Newcastle Quayside 1994. (M. Blenkinsop.)

Plate 7. Newcastle Quayside 1996. (M. Blenkinsop.)

Plate 8.
The mouth of the River Tyne in 198.
The Albert Edward Dock is on the
Tyne's north bank and nearby the s
of TWDC's Royal Quays Developmer
(AirFotos.)

Plate 9.
The Royal Quays Development in
1997 showing new housing, roads
and, close to the middle roundabout,
the Twining's tea factory. The Wet
'n' Wild Water Park is below the
Twining's factory and above the
recently constructed Retail Centres.
(AirFotos.)

Plate 10.
New homes being built at North Dock, River Wear in 1996. The Marine Activities Centre was built for local residents and the North Dock houses a new marina. (Chris Henderson.)

Plate 11.
The mouth of the River Wear in 1991 prior to the TWDC's St Peter's Riverside Development. (AirFotos.)

Plate 12.
The St Peter's Riverside Development. To the east of St Peter's Church, on the north bank of the Wear, is St Peter's Campus, Sunderland University. Opposite the Campus, and running along the river's south bank, is student housing and the recently restored Roseline Building. There are yachts berthed in the new marina in North Dock. (AirFotos.)

from the Wear went via the Hetton Colliery Railway staithes.

The widespread introduction of coal staithes and the deepening of the two rivers marked the end of the Tyne and Wear keelmen whose keels had carried coal from the upstream mines down to the anchored colliers in the river mouths since the fourteenth century. The efficiencies introduced by the increasing use of staithes, railways and steamship colliers meant that the North East coal exports could keep up with demand. Coal exports from the Tyne increased from around 3.8 million tons in 1850 to over 20 million tons in 1913. On the Wear coal exports rose from 119,960 tons in 1854 to exceed 5 million tons by 1904.

It was inevitable that a nationwide network of *public* railways should follow the early private colliery railways. Government approval was given for a public railway in 1821 and George Stephenson left the Killingworth Colliery to oversee the building of a line that ran from Witton Park Colliery, near Bishop Auckland, through Darlington to Stockton on the Tees. In 1825 the world's first public railway came into existence when one of Stephenson's locomotives, or 'travelling steam engines', was attached to 38 wagons loaded with coal and merchandise and carriages with some 450 passengers. The initial part of the voyage with George Stephenson and his brothers on the footplate was perceived as a great success when the locomotive and its load travelled to Darlington at speeds that in some places approached 15 miles per hour. At Darlington more coal wagons were added and, complete with some 600 passengers, the locomotive

successfully completed the trip to Stockton. By 1829 George Stephenson's *Rocket* was travelling on the Liverpool Manchester line at 36 miles per hour. The railway age had arrived and turnpike roads and canals were doomed as during the next 30 years most of Britain's main railway lines were laid.

The building of the bridges at Newcastle is a measure of the development of the industrialisation of the North East. In 1831 a suspension bridge was built near Scotswood and in 1839 the first Scotswood railway bridge was constructed. From Roman times, until the High Level bridge was built in 1849, there had only been one bridge across the river at Newcastle. The Redheugh bridge was built in 1871 and the low-arched Tyne bridge replaced by a swing bridge in 1876. The King Edward Bridge was opened in 1906 and in 1928 the graceful arches of the Tyne Bridge were completed. (The Redheugh bridge was replaced in 1983, and in 1981 the Queen Elizabeth II Metro Bridge was opened.)

After the railways came the iron-hulled steamships. The first steamships were powered by steam engines mounted inside wooden hulls. The first Tyne-built steamship was the *Rapid* which was able to steam from Newcastle to London in 56 hours in 1824. Three years later the steamship *Hylton Jolliffe* began a regular summer service to London. The first all-iron steamship built on the Tyne was the *Prince Albert* which was launched from Coutt's yard at Walker in 1842. The first screw-driven ship from the North East was the iron-hulled collier, the *John Bowes*, which was launched in 1852 from Palmer's yard at Jarrow. This was a

The launch of the John Bowes. (Illustrated London News).

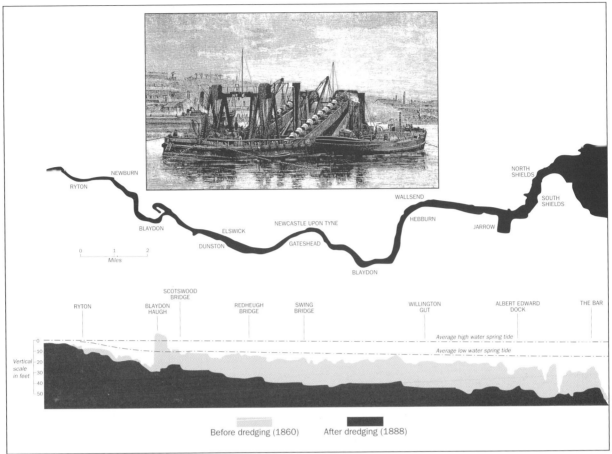

RYTON
NEWBURN
BLAYDON
ELSWICK
DUNSTON
NEWCASTLE UPON TYNE
GATESHEAD
BLAYDON
WALLSEND
HEBBURN
JARROW
NORTH SHIELDS
SOUTH SHIELDS

0   1   2
Miles

SCOTSWOOD BRIDGE
RYTON
BLAYDON HAUGH
REDHEUGH BRIDGE
SWING BRIDGE
WILLINGTON GUT
ALBERT EDWARD DOCK
THE BAR

Average high water spring tide
Average low water spring tide

Vertical scale in feet

Before dredging (1860)   After dredging (1888)

The Dredging of the Tyne. Inset: Steam Dredger.

momentous event that was to end the days of the famous bluff-bowed, wooden-hulled nineteenth century wooden collier, the 'Geordie brig'. As sail slowly gave way to steam, the brig's three head sails, two masts, each square rigged with a mainsail and topsail, and an additional fore and aft spanker on the second mast, were replaced by the more efficient marine steam engine.

The screw-driven, iron-hulled *John Bowes* was also fitted with revolutionary 'double-bottom tanks' that were built into the underwater section of the hull. These tanks could be filled with sea water ballast and solved one of the greatest problems to navigation in the Tyne and the Wear – the shallowing of the river due to the dumping overboard of solid ballast. For centuries colliers had sailed outward from the Tyne and Wear and returned in ballast. Sand ballast was sometimes used for local industries, like the glass industry, but it was mostly gravel shovelled out of the hold into the river. For centuries seamen had been fined for illegally dumping ballast – as early as 1655 there were complaints about ballast silting in the Tyne and by 1765 the Tyne had *'so deteriorated through neglect and the dropping overboard of ballast that*

where the ships used to load and lie afloat at low water was then dry in several places' (Hodgson). By the mid 1850s there were over 30 screw-driven, iron colliers with double bottomed tanks exporting Newcastle coal and returning with sea-water filled, double-bottomed tanks which were pumped out before the ship was refilled with coal. But, by then, it was too late. The Tyne had become so shallow that it was almost unnavigable and desperately needed to be deepened.

With their customary vigour the Victorians went to work. The power Newcastle had had over the river since James I was relinquished when in 1850 the Tyne Navigation Act was passed and total control of the river's navigation passed over to a Tyne Improvement Commission which was made up of 18 members: two from Gateshead, three each from North and South Shields, six from the Newcastle Corporation and four from the Admiralty. The Commissioner's first act was to build two massive piers at the river mouth so as to protect the entrance and to help scour and deepen the channel. Work started in 1854 and after numerous failures and wall breaches by severe gales the piers were finally completed in

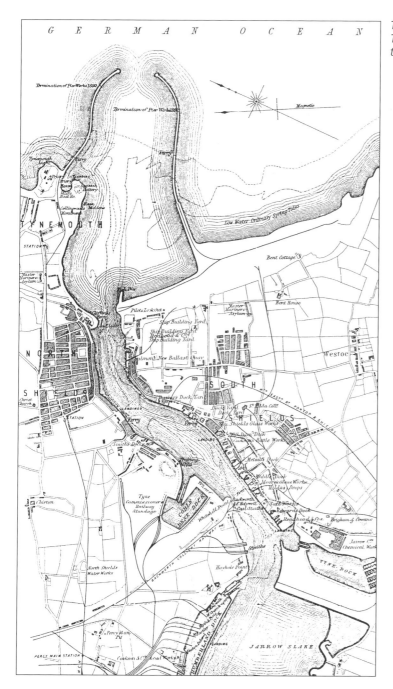

The mouth of the Tyne in 1881 and the new docks.

The Tyne entrance today: North and South Piers.

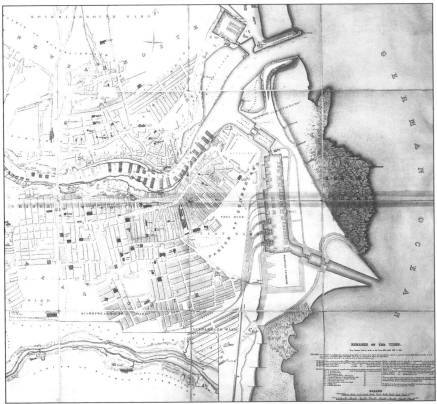

Map drawn in 1853 of Sunderland, Bishopwearmouth and Monkwearmouth. The North Dock was opened in 1837 by the Wearmouth Dock Company and Sunderland South Dock was opened in 1850 by the Sunderland Dock Company.

world and could simultaneously load more than 16 colliers from its four staithes and 42 spouts.

Navigation in the Wear was also seriously hampered by the dumping of ballast as well as the added danger of overcrowded anchorages in the lower reaches. The River Wear Commissioners (who were directly responsible for keeping the river navigable, page 98) vigorously pursued and fined colliers which dumped ballast in the river. The North and South piers were constantly maintained and improved and the river deepened by steam dredging – by the world's first steam-driven

1895. The newly-invented steam dredgers scooped millions of tons of material from the bottom of the river and carried it out to sea so that the lower reaches were deep enough to take ocean steamers up to Newcastle Quay and to float warships from the shipyards at Elswick. Whitehall Point and Bill Point were completely cut away and at Lemington the channel was straightened so that the tidal flow was carried inland to Hedwin Streams. In addition the Northumberland Dock, Tyne Dock and Albert Edward Dock were constructed. The Northumberland Dock was built by the Tyne Commission for the coal mines north of the Tyne, while Tyne Dock and the newly constructed east and west Dunston Staithes served the pits and railway network to the south. Tyne Dock exported more coal than any other dock in the

dredgers – to such an extent that by 1817: *'the sands and rocks on an exposed coast at the mouth of the River Wear had given way to a safe and commodious harbour with its entrance piers and lighthouse and a deep channel maintained by steam dredging'* (Milburn & Miller). The opening of Seaham harbour in 1831 (see below) was a

The first collier leaves Sunderland South Dock, May 1850. (Illustrated London News).

direct threat to the Sunderland coal trade and steps were taken by the Commissioners to improve the Wear's facilities. The North pier was extended during the 1830s and in 1841 the old octagonal lighthouse (page 109) moved to its new position at the end of the extension. The Commissioners consultant, Robert Stephenson, suggested the building of a dock on the south bank of the Wear which had the best access for the colliery railways of the Durham coalfield but Sir Hedworth Williamson, a County Durham MP, sponsored the development of a North Dock on his land at Monkwearmouth. The North Dock, completed in 1837, was too small and the entrance not easily accessible. George Hudson, the so-called 'railway king' from York, was invited to stand for Parliament on condition that he improved the situation. He was elected as Sunderland's MP, lobbied government for help, saved the recently-formed Dock and Railway Company from bankruptcy and pressed for a new dock on the south bank. In 1850 the huge South Dock was opened which could accommodate over 250 vessels and was then the largest dock in Britain. It was not long before the railways linked the Port of Sunderland to the new local pits and the many distant coal mines of the Durham coalfield.

Throughout the nineteenth century River Wear Commissioners fulfilled their obligations by continuing to dredge the main channel

Meik's iron lighthouse. Thomas Meik engineered Hendon Dock as a southern extension to Sunderland South Dock or Hudson Dock as it later became known. Meik's lighthouse was moved to Roker seafront in 1983.

The mouth of the Wear from North Dock, c. 1880. On the end of South Pier is Thomas Meik's cast iron lighthouse which was built in 1856. The North Pier lighthouse was destroyed in 1902.

The 2,800 feet (853.4 metres) long northern breakwater, Roker Pier, built of concrete blocks faced with granite. The two, massive, outer breakwaters (Roker Pier and New South Pier) were the River Wear Commissioners' last great projects.

£1 million. Nowhere in England was a town so dependent on merchant shipbuilding in the period of the Industrial Revolution and the town could readily justify its claim to be the 'first shipbuilding port in the world', launching ships for some 14 different nations.

The yards on the Wear were usually family concerns and on a single site there was often all the necessary skills to build a wooden ship: from shipwright to sail maker. By 1860 iron ship building was overtaking the wooden tonnage and world-famous yards like Doxford, Austin, Laing and Pickersgill dominated Sunderland's shipbuilding industry. By 1914 Sunderland was launching some 300,000 tons of shipping and

and, between 1864 and 1868, developing the Hendon Dock to improve the river's loading facilities. During the 1870s and 80s all the dock entrances were widened to accommodate the larger ships visiting the port. Breakwaters were constructed by the Commissioners on either side of the piers and work began on Roker Pier in 1885. On completion in 1902 it was 2,800ft long and the distinct red and white granite lighthouse at the end of the pier, which became operational in 1903, was then Britain's most powerful lighthouse. In 1893 work was started on the south breakwater and continued through until 1912.

With deeper, more navigable rivers the way was clear for rapid expansion of shipbuilding on the Wear and the Tyne. The first steam tug was built in 1825 on the Wear but although there was generally less shipbuilding innovation from the Wear shipyards (when compared to those on the Tyne) more wooden tonnage was produced. At the end of the Napoleonic Wars there were some two dozen yards on the Wear. This increased to over 60 in the 1830s only to crash in the 'hungry 40s' to around 30. By the 1850s there were over 40 incredibly productive yards which produced one-third of Britain's merchant shipping tonnage. In 1821 Sunderland produced 11% of the total British tonnage. This had increased to 25% by 1830 and to an astonishing 38% by mid century. By 1855 wooden shipbuilding supported the people of Sunderland where ship production was estimated to be worth

The red and white Aberdeen granite lighthouse at the end of Roker Pier. When the lighthouse was built in 1903 it was Britain's most powerful navigational light.

A busy River Wear c. 1875 and the rebuilt iron bridge. The original iron bridge was built under the supervision of Roland Burdon MP and Thomas Wilson and rebuilt by Robert Stephenson in 1859. Stephenson's bridge was replaced by the road bridge in 1929. The funnel shaped glass works off Lambton Staithes were destroyed when the 'hog back' railway bridge was constructed in 1879. The moored ships show the transition from sail to steam with funnels and fore and aft sails.

Today's Wear bridges. In the foreground is the 'hog back' railway bridge which, when built in 1879, was the largest girder bridge in the world. In the background is the 1929 Road Bridge.

nearly half of the work force was working in shipbuilding or related industries.

On the Tyne shipbuilding innovation abounded and men like Palmer, Armstrong and Parsons were some the world's greatest industrialists who, in the second half of the nineteenth century, took the region and Tyneside to unprecedented prosperity. In 1872 Charles Palmer's yard at Jarrow, which launched the *John Bowes*, built the world's first oil tanker, the *Vaterland*. This innovative yard developed a process of rolling armour plates and the *Terror* was one of the first iron warships built for the Admiralty. Just before the First World War this yard was producing massive

Armstrong's Elswick works c. 1887.

Dreadnought battleships as tension flared between empire-building Germany and Britain. In 1903 Swan, Hunter and Richardson shipbuilding yard was created and from 1903 to 1913 built an average of 93,000 tons a year, launching in 1907 the Cunard liner, the *Mauretania*, which was then the largest and fastest vessel in the world.

On the Tyne heavy engineering companies and shipyards tended to combine and firms like Armstrong's of Elswick were typical of such highly successful ventures. William Armstrong was born in Newcastle and was an inventive genius. In 1844 he invented the 'hydroelectric machine' for electricity generation and developed hydraulic-driven machines, such as hydraulic cranes, at his Elswick works. In 1855 he invented a revolutionary field gun and in 1882 he designed the Admiralty's first gunboat which was built at Mitchell's Walker yard. He

amalgamated his engineering works with Mitchell's shipyards to create the Armstrong Mitchell's yards. Merchant ships were built at the Walker yard and warships at a newly constructed yard at Elswick. Steel works were added to the Armstrong empire and, when he died in 1900, his works occupied over 230 acres, employed some 25,000 men and formed the largest industrial empire in Europe.

George Stephenson died in 1848 in Chesterfield. His son Robert, one of Britain's greatest civil engineers, stayed in Newcastle and continued building engines at their Forth Street factory until his death in 1859. The Hawthorn brothers, also pioneers of locomotives, had workshops in Forth Street and, in 1885, amalgamated with Leslie to become R. and W. Hawthorn Leslies's and, buying up the Stephenson's Forth Street workshops, the company went on to become one of the world's most famous manufacturing companies building ships, marine engines and locomotives. Stephenson's and Hawthorn Leslie later merged in the 1930s during the Depression.

Charles Parsons invented the steam turbine in 1884 and the first turbine developed some seven and half kilowatts of power and was used to provide ship's lighting. He also successfully combined Tyneside engineering and shipbuilding skills when in 1894 Parson's Heaton engineering works and his Marine Steam Turbine Company at Wallsend built the experimental vessel the *Turbinia* which was fitted with the world's first steam turbine engine. In 1897, during the naval review commemorating Queen Victoria's Diamond Jubilee, this 100 foot steam-turbine-driven vessel created a sensation by roaring through the two lines of battleships at the then unheard speed of 34.5 knots. Just ten years after *Turbinia* had swept through the fleet, the record-breaking Cunard liner, the *Mauretania*, was launched from the Swan Hunter and Richardson yard and, powered by Parsons' steam turbine engines, became the fastest ship in the world,

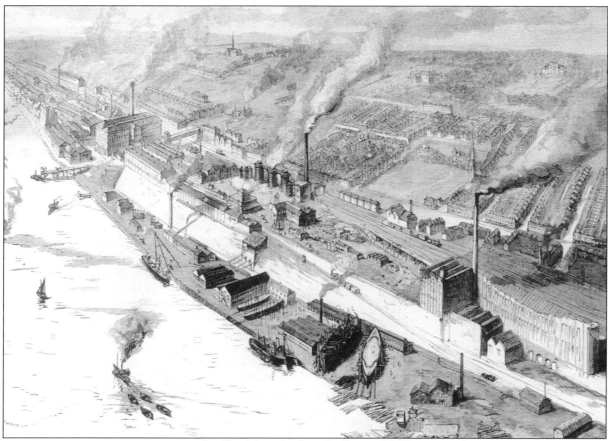

The Elswick works from the Tyne c. 1900.

winning the coveted *Blue Ribbon* prize for crossing the North Atlantic in less than five days. The new *Dreadnought* class of battleships that were developed by the Admiralty in the pre-First World War naval armaments race with Germany were also powered by steam turbines.

Towards the end of the nineteenth century there was a rise in the region's timber import industry for pit props and railway sleepers and, to help feed the rapidly-expanding population, there was a rapid development of steam driven grain mills. But by 1914 three major industries dominated the banks of the Tyne and Wear – coal export, heavy engineering and shipbuilding – and they led to the decline of many non-associated riverside industries such as pottery, glass, soap and iron production. As the First World War approached the region was probably the wealthiest part of the richest country in the world. But after the war the North East was to pay for this massive increase and concentration of its resources in heavy industry.

Electricity production was stimulated in the region by Sunderland-born Joseph Swan's almost simultaneous invention (with that of Edison's in America) of the electric light bulb in his home laboratory in Gateshead. He gave a public demonstration of the light bulb at the Newcastle Literary and Philosophical Society in 1880. Newcastle had the first British street to be lit by electricity and a factory, the first in Europe, was built in South Benwell to make electric lamps. Charles Parsons' invention of the world's first turbo-dynamo for electricity generation in 1884 led to the development of huge turbo-alternators for the production of electricity at power stations. Slowly local industries converted from steam and coal to electricity generated in coal-fired power stations. The twentieth century had arrived and with its arrival, along with the wireless telegraph, electric light, cars and aeroplanes, came the First World War. Britain won the war but never recovered its former economic glory.

CHAPTER TWELVE

THE TWENTIETH CENTURY: wars and recession (1914-1997)

The twentieth century opened with Britain arguably the greatest of the world superpowers and the head of a huge empire. From its nineteenth century position as the 'workplace of the world' Britain descended to being described as the economic 'sick man of Europe' before gradually coming to terms with the loss of the Empire, a much-reduced international role and the country's technical backwardness and slowness in developing late twentieth century working and manufacturing practices. The twentieth century is America's century and, following the collapse of Communism, America is currently the world's only superpower. During this tumultuous century Britain twice declared war on Germany and twice America followed suit to bring her enormous reserves of manpower and resources to help win the wars that raged across the globe.

In 1914, following the defeat of France by Germany in the Franco-Prussian war, Britain went to war against imperial German expansionism, although the immediate cause of war was the conflict of interest between Russia and the Austro-Hungarians in the Balkans. The German forces rapidly made their way through Belgium but were halted by the British Expeditionary Force and the French at the battle of Marne. German attempts to reach the Channel were again thwarted at the battle of Ypres and, as the armies dug in, the conflict became the terrible trench warfare that characterised World War I.

The Germans fought the war on the Western Front against the British and French and on the Eastern Front against Russia, who advanced into Prussia. Turkey attacked Russia and the Gallipoli campaign was fought mainly by Australian and New Zealand soldiers against the Turks. The Russian Revolution in 1917 was in part due to the failure of the Allies to relieve Russia. Fighting took place in the Middle East and in Italy and a decisive moment was when the USA entered the war in 1917. An exhausted Germany was eventually defeated on the Western front by the British, French and Americans. The other Central Powers, the Austro-Hungarians, the Turks and Bulgarians also capitulated. When the Treaty of Versailles was signed in 1919 in Paris the Allies had lost five million lives and the Central Powers some three and a half million. Despite the terrible suffering, deaths and deprivations that the soldiers suffered during the four years of trench warfare, remarkably, the 1914-18 war remained a popular cause with most of the British public.

In the opening stages of the war, and regardless of the effects on neutral nations, Britain mined the North Sea. Germany retaliated by declaring the seas around Britain and Ireland a 'war zone'. It soon became total war when troops were gassed, citizens shelled and bombed from the air and warships and submarines sank defenceless merchantmen and commandeered neutral shipping. The British Fleet was based in Scapa Flow relatively safe from the German submarine menace and, from a distance, blockaded the German ports. The German surface fleet only emerged once and then the giant battleships of each side fought the bloody but inconclusive Battle of Jutland in 1916 where, in less than one hour, 25 ships were destroyed and some 10,000 men died. The German fleet returned to port to be blockaded by the British war-fleet for the rest of the war. Early in the war Germany quickly realised the value of submarines which were cheaper and more deadly than the huge battleships and Britain was unprepared to fight them. Germany's small submarine fleet sank some seven million tons of commercial shipping and Britain, who no longer fed herself, had only a few weeks supplies of food left when America entered the war. Once at war America rapidly built up her merchant fleet with the dual intention of developing as a maritime power and aiding Britain by relieving the submarine blockade. America's industrial power was such that by the end of the war

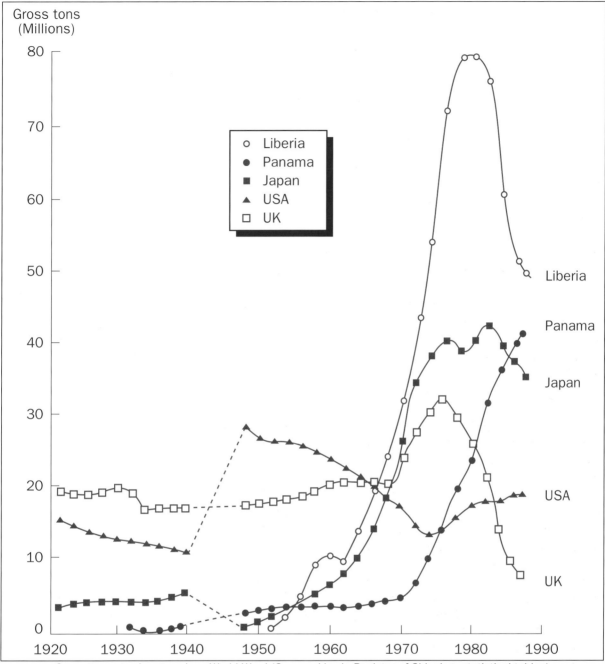

Gross tons (Millions)

Gross tonnage changes since World War I (Source: Lloyds Register of Shipping, statistical tables).

merchant shipping production had grown four-fold, more than sufficient to relieve the submarine blockade of Britain. By 1919 Britain still had the world's largest merchant fleet, about 16 million tons gross, but America, with 10 million tons, was in second place.

Prior to the outbreak of the 1914-18 war Britain was not at peace with itself. The trade union movement was growing, industrial unrest was increasing, there was serious trouble in Ireland and dissent in the colonies, particularly India. Coal miners, railwaymen and transport workers threatened to combine to bring the country to a standstill as the

railwaymen fought for union recognition. But with the outbreak of war, British people of all classes and the countries of the Empire united. As the country switched from a peace to a war economy industry prospered, especially those in the North East which now depended on shipbuilding, armaments and heavy engineering. Victorian *laissez-faire* died as the State took control of industry and the economy. Men went to war and many women worked in factories and essential industries – over a million women were employed around the country by 1918. With the commitment of all classes to the 1914-1918 war effort, Britain underwent a social and economic revolution and for a while the 'class system' relaxed. In 1918 the Fourth Reform Bill was passed to give manhood suffrage and votes to women over 30. Britain was to be a land fit for the returning heroes. But it was not to last.

The war ended and the State gave back the major industries to their owners. The class system re-emerged in British society, but there were important post war changes, not least some emancipation for women. Lloyd George as Prime Minister (1916-1922) and a Liberal and Tory coalition government legislated for improved elementary education, state housing for the poor, unemployment insurance and better public health. By 1919 the trade union movement had doubled its membership to some eight million and workers' wages went up. Lloyd George's government bloodily and ineffectually pursued the IRA between 1919 and 1921 and he finally conceded in 1921 an independent Irish Free State composed of 26 Catholic counties in the south and six Protestant counties in the north, which remained part of the United Kingdom. He fell from power in 1922 and a divided Liberal party lost its way as Tory and Labour parties dominated British politics for the rest of the century.

There was a huge increase in national debt as a result of World War I. Britain's extensive overseas investments had to be sold and there was a loss of foreign markets and a general industrial decline that led to increasing unemployment, especially in the North. There was a short post-war shipping boom that lasted until 1920. But the economic disruption caused by the war and a massive over-production of ships as governments subsidised the building of merchant fleets (often as part of national maritime policy) caused the price of ships and freights to drop. British ship production, in terms of tonnage, did not fall between 1914 and 1933 and was one of the major causes of the 1920s and 1930s overproduction.

Southern Britain in the 1920s and 30s was relatively prosperous but in the North it was a period of increasing unemployment and poverty as the traditional industries – steel-making, ship-building, heavy engineering and railways – declined from loss of markets, overseas competition and lack of capital investment. The government's return to the

Pelaw Main Staithes, Bill Quay on the Tyne: shipyards and the transition from sail to steam. Steam dredgers, coal drops, moored collier brigantines and steam tramp ships. Coal-fired tramp ships were the mainstay of the highly successful British shipping industry.

gold standard in 1925 meant that British coal and steel exports were over-valued. As the Northern British economy floundered, 'class war' resurfaced which led to the 1926 general strike when the government refused to continue a subsidy to the coal mining industry. The American stock exchange crashed in 1929 and the British Labour government could do little as world trade declined and Britain's uncompetitive, traditional Northern industries failed. By 1932 there were some three million unemployed workers and the famous, peaceful Jarrow march in 1936 was mainly made up of shipyard workers protesting against high local unemployment and poverty and did much to alert the more prosperous South to the conditions in the Northern shipbuilding towns. The close-knit working class communities, with their working mens' clubs, pigeons, pubs, football, plus a benign welfare state (*laissez-faire* was long dead) probably all helped to prevent the situation in Northern Britain from becoming revolutionary. The stagnant Northern industrial regions were designated 'special areas' for some limited 'National government' (which was dominated by the Conservatives) help, but only when the country began to re-arm after 1935 was there any significant improvement. During the 1930s depression the Midlands and South were relatively affluent and unaffected as light consumer industries – electrical, chemical, textile, motor car and service – grew in a time of low inflation, falling prices and cheap private housing. It was the period in which the country's wealth-producing region shifted from the North to the South.

On the continent in the 1930s totalitarianism swept through Austria, Spain, Italy and Germany. Germany, Italy and Japan built up their merchant and naval fleets as part of the expansionist policies of totalitarian regimes. For centuries Britain had shown the world that control of the ocean trading routes and sea trade were essential elements in any expansionist philosophy. As early as 1925 Germany was exporting more ships than

Britain. In the 1930s Japan started off on a mercurial rise that was eventually to make the country one of the world's major ship builders and owners. World tonnage rose (a significant fraction made up of oil tankers), despite the serious slump in world trade, from 50 million tons in 1924 to 68 million tons in 1933, the worst year of the economic depression, to reach 65.5 million tons just before World War II.

Britain, whose coal and iron resources were the corner stones of her nineteenth century world supremacy, was a country without oil and slower than most of the rapidly industrialising

Post-war general cargo ships, like the Coromandel *built in 1949, where often powered by Sunderland built Doxford diesels. These oil-fired ships soon replaced the steam tramp ships.*

countries to change over to the new energy source despite its many advantages. The developed world slowly entered the 'petroleum age' and oil began to replace coal as the new primary energy source. In 1902, for example, only 1% of the world's merchant shipping used oil to make steam but by 1918 this had increased to 15%. The fast, post-war, Atlantic passenger-liners were some of the first ships to be converted from coal to oil-burning. Oil-fired burners were more efficient and less labour intensive at producing steam than coal-fired burners. Further, oil could be pumped aboard, took up only one third of the hull space and could be stored in 'double bottom tanks' (page 124). Up to the 1950s coal was the most important fuel source for British industry but then it was quickly overtaken by the availability of cheap Middle Eastern oil. Other countries like Germany and Poland opened up extensive, easily-mined coalfields. Cheap foreign oil and coal were detrimental to the British economy, especially in the North.

Huge container ships, built in the Far East, quickly brought about the demise of the British shipping industry.

The two main causes of World War II were the failure of the 1919 Treaty of Versailles to maintain international security and the aggressive, territorial ambitions of Adolf Hitler who marched into the Rhineland in 1936. After the German invasion of Bohemia-Moravia in 1939, Britain and France agreed to support Poland and when Hitler invaded Poland (with Soviet troops after Hitler had formed an alliance with USSR in 1939), France and Britain declared war on Germany. German submarine activity against commercial shipping again almost brought Britain to the brink of defeat and, once again, America entered the war at a crucial moment and helped bring about victory. Hitler invaded the USSR in 1941, his attempts to invade Britain thwarted by the RAF and the English Channel. Britain for much of 1940 and 1941 had stood alone against the German war machine. Japan, driven by a desire for expansion and a concern about economic sanctions, attacked the American naval base at Pearl Harbor in 1941. America immediately declared war on Japan. The war ended in 1945 with the fall of Berlin and the German collapse in Italy. Germany lost some three and half million combatants, Britain and the Commonwealth over half a million, America over a quarter of a million, Japan two million and the Soviet Union a staggering 11 million. Nearly seven million

people were murdered in Nazi concentration camps, some six million of them Jews. Millions of civilians died during the fighting, especially in Russia and Germany.

By 1950, through effective mass-production techniques, America had increased its total merchant fleet from a prewar figure of 11.4 million tons gross to nearly 27.5 million tons. Britain had gained about a million gross tons, bringing its total tonnage to 18.2 million, despite the British Empire having lost 60% of its merchant fleet during the war (page 133). In the post-war period international trade made a quick recovery and a shipping boom continued well into the 1950s.

The returning British soldiers, sailors and airmen wanted a better, more egalitarian society and this time they got one. The trade unions were now very powerful. Ernest Bevin, the leader of the Transport and General Workers Union, was appointed Minister of Labour in 1940 and played a major role in Churchill's administration, as had many other Labour members. A few days after the German surrender in 1945 Churchill's Conservative-Labour coalition collapsed as the Labour ministers left the government. In the general election the Labour Party, led by Clement Attlee, was returned with a huge majority on an election platform that promised industrial regeneration, full employment and public health and housing. For six years Labour Party legislation improved welfare and developed a mixed economy. All the major industries were nationalised (some 20% of the nation's industry) and the National Health Service came into effect in 1948. National insurance, along with state grammar schools and council houses, all contributed to the 'welfare state'. In the post war boom wages rose, there was full employment and improved leisure activities. The Conservatives, in power from 1951 to 1964, kept to the middle political ground and there were few strikes and little national unrest.

The war had left Britain with a vast debt and the country became more-inward looking. There was neither the will nor the money to control its enormous bloc of overseas possessions and the British Empire was gradually disbanded from the late 1940s through the 1950s and 60s. The North Atlantic Treaty Organisation (NATO) was formed in 1949 binding Britain, America, Belgium, France, Canada, Italy, the Netherlands and a number of other countries to see an armed attack on one nation as an attack on all. NATO was formed to counter any communist USSR expansionism in Western Europe and West Germany joined in 1955.

In 1964 Harold Wilson was elected Prime Minister of a British Labour government (1964-1970). In the mid to late 1960s there were British, Continental and American anti-war protests against the American involvement in the Vietnam War (1964-1974) where, by 1968, over half a million American troops were involved in the fight to support the non-Communist south against the Communist north. The protests, often led by students, became increasingly violent.

The British economy suffered as overseas markets were gradually lost, productivity was relatively low and its industries and industrial practices were outdated. The result was a balance of payments crisis, high inflation, devaluation and unemployment which began to grow at an alarming rate with the old industrial regions of the North suffering most. Strikes mounted as the powerful unions flexed their muscles. The miners' strike in 1974, during Edward Heath's Conservative government, reduced the country to a three-day working-week and the resulting general election returned a marginal Labour government. By 1974 British coal was no longer competitive and the cost of oil (the world's main energy source) soared as Middle Eastern oil producers increased prices by some 400%.

The declining British economy at this time of high energy costs was set against a general slump in world trade. The slump was further aggravated by the decolonisation programmes of the 1950s and 60s which brought many new nations into world trade, all eager to own and build their own merchant fleets. There was massive over-production of world shipping that was made worse by several factors: government subsidies to the shipyards of Scandinavian, European and Far Eastern countries; the developing countries insisting on carrying their own cargoes (as Britain had in Cromwell's time); American protectionism of its coastal ships and the USSR continuing to over-produce a large state-owned merchant fleet. Tanker over-production was especially bad and further aggravated by the oil price increases. Marginally-subsidised British shipbuilding was unable to compete – the price of the steel to build a ship in a British yard was more than the final cost of the same ship built in the Far East! Shipbuilding was further threatened as air travel began to vie with sea transport. In 1945 the passenger liner *Queen Elizabeth* made her maiden voyage, but by 1958 the number of passengers carried by air across the Atlantic exceeded those carried by sea. By the 1960s cheap air travel had virtually finished off the transatlantic passenger trade.

A feature of post-World War II shipping was the rapid rise of 'flags of convenience' tonnage, where ships were registered in different countries from the nationality of the owners. Britain's merchant fleet, once the world's largest, declined as ships 'went foreign'. The great advantage to shipowners was that they paid less tax on the high earnings during the world trade boom years of the 1950s. Convenience ships were also freed from stringent shipping legislation, owners could employ cheaper labour and safety legislation was often less demanding (although the safety records of convenience ships was not markedly different to those of the more established maritime nations). Today the tonnage of ships registered under the British flag is about one tenth of that registered under the Liberian flag.

Merchant shipping underwent a revolution in 1965 when *Sealand* introduced containerisation on the North Atlantic shipping lanes. The end of the conventional port and cargo ship was in sight as, from the 1960s until the 1980s, world shipping and trade underwent a massive change, almost similar to the replacement of sail by steam that had occurred during the same years in the previous century. New types of ships, new practices, new ports, and Far Eastern shipbuilders broke the hold of traditional maritime nations. Britain suffered the most, losing thousands of seafarers, hundreds of ships and tens of companies and yards. The dockyards of traditional 'break-bulk' ports such as Glasgow, Liverpool, Cardiff, London and Newcastle decayed as custom-built container ports, like Felixstowe and Southampton, were rapidly constructed to berth the revolutionary ships.

One by one the shipyards and coal mines of Britain began to close. In the 1970s inflation went out of control and by the early 1980s unemployment soared to over three million, exceeding the worst days of the 1930s depression. Britain entered the Common Market in 1973, after being rejected by France in 1963, but Brussels had little effect on Britain's continued economic decline and social unrest. 'Social contracts' between Labour governments (1974-1979) and the trade union movement produced an uneasy peace until 1979 when a strike bound 'winter of discontent' helped a Conservative government, led by Margaret Thatcher, to become elected. There was high unemployment and industrial recession but by the following year Britain was at least self-sufficient in North Sea oil. In 1982 there was an outburst of jingoism when Margaret Thatcher crushed an Argentinean invasion of the distant Falkland Islands.

The year-long miners' strike of 1984 split the National Union of Miners and hastened the closure of even more pits. Britain's primary energy source finally switched from coal to oil, gas and nuclear power. The economy greatly benefited from the North Sea oil and the change to modern light industries and working practices. An economic revival followed, fuelled by a consumer boom, easy credit and booming service industries, especially in the South. State industries were privatised and anti-trade union legislation completed Margaret Thatcher's popular vision of individual 'self-reliance' and an enterprise-culture based on a house and share-owning democracy. Her appeal was wide: in 1980 trade union membership was some 13 million; by 1987 it had dropped to around nine million. Victorian *laissez-faire* was no longer a dirty word but as quickly as the economy boomed out of the early 1980s it dropped back into recession in the early 1990s with a fall in house prices that was to result in 'negative equity' and hardship for many new houseowners. Re-elected for a third term in 1987, 'Thatcherite' politics and an economic policy based on monetarism ran out of steam. A deeply unpopular poll tax, internal rows over Europe, National Health 'privatisation' and a massive balance of payments deficit brought about Margaret Thatcher's downfall. The Tory party backbenchers elected a milder replacement in John Major. The Gulf War helped revive a flagging Tory party's fortunes but Major's government became extremely unpopular, despite a period of economic growth accompanied with low interest rates and low inflation. In May 1997 the new Labour party were elected with a large majority to form a government under Tony Blair.

In the late twentieth century Britain's material wealth is higher than ever before even with the distressing feature of many long-term unemployed. Manufacturing is far less important in the overall economy as financial, service and light industries replace the traditional coal, steel, shipbuilding and heavy industries. Britain's future path is unsure as some look uneasily to Europe and the European Union while others believe the path to be an 'offshore enterprise culture'. Only time will tell.

Two Rivers

There was discontent among the North East workforce as World War I loomed and as part of the social unrest that marked the prewar period in British history. There were threats of strikes in the Tyne and Wear coalfields as the miners became concerned about the loss of export markets and the transport workers were threatening to halt the region's trams. But when war was declared in 1914 the men of Tyneside and Wearside flocked to their local recruitment offices. Local battalions were raised and the men went off to war, cheered by their wives and girlfriends, many of whom would soon play an important part in the local war effort.

The First World War was a popular cause with much of the British population. Details from the Newcastle War Memorial at Barras Bridge.

At the beginning of the war the Tyne and Wear shipyards were taken over by the State and the Ministry of Shipping was responsible for all aspects of British shipbuilding. Some 18,000 Sunderland men went to war, many of them skilled shipyard workers. To help keep the shipyards operating at full strength women entered the yards. By the end of the war, the Wearsiders had produced nearly one million tons of merchant shipping – mostly coal-fired, 'three-island' tramp steamers – although some warships were also produced, Doxfords building 21 torpedo boat destroyers. On the Tyne women also worked side by side with the men as the traditional shipbuilding, heavy engineering, armaments and coal-mining industries stepped up production. The gigantic Armstrong works on the Tyne, for example, whose annual profits rose to £1 million during the war, was employing some 17,000 women by 1918 (page 142). There may have been a shortage of food but there was never a shortage of work as the Germans stepped up their submarine campaign against British merchant shipping. Wages doubled during the war and although there were local scares as

Zeppelins attacked the region, dropping bombs on Wallsend and Sunderland (22 people were killed and over 100 injured in a Zeppelin raid on Sunderland in 1916), the region greatly prospered. But prosperity was not to last.

The 1919 Treaty of Versailles which was followed by the Washington Conference in 1921 imposed strict arms control on the countries of Europe to the serious detriment of the industries of the North East. Henry Mess, writing about Industrial Tyneside in 1928, well describes the post war situation: *'When the War came, it stimulated still further the shipbuilding and ship repairing industries and the armament industry. Tyneside became a huge arsenal and dock-yard. In the couple of years of trade boom after the Armistice there was a further delirious expansion of shipbuilding, whilst at one time incredibly high prices were paid for coal shipments. Then came the steepest slump on record, with heavy losses and appalling unemployment.'*

The fall of the combined output of the numbers of ships (ships were getting larger) being built in Sunderland's shipyards gives a clear measure of the progress of the dramatic

Previous page and above: Guns and shells were produced by the millions at the Vickers-Armstrong works.
Below: Women at work in the Vickers-Armstrong works in 1916. They made an extremely important contribution to the war effort and some 17,000 were in employment at the works by 1918.

decline of regional shipbuilding. In 1920 sixteen Wearside yards produced 67 ships; this dropped to 16 ships in 1923 and eight by the remaining 13 yards in 1926. By then there were some 19,000 Sunderland men out of work. A mini-boom followed but by 1929 it was over and for the next five years the number of ships built was dismal. On the Tyne things were just as bad. The mighty Armstrong yards, for example, built only one warship between 1920 and 1936.

Technology was changing to the disadvantage of the coal-fired British tramp ships. The German engineer Rudolf Diesel (1858-1913) developed his oil-fired internal-combustion engine which as 'marine diesels' successfully powered the German World War I submarine: the 90 year old monopoly of the coal-powered, reciprocating steam-engine was over. As early as 1906 William Doxford's Sunderland yard had begun to consider diesel engines as a means of propulsion. In 1921, after years of research, the yard successfully launched the *Yngaren*, powered by a 3,000 horse-power Doxford diesel. Soon merchant ships throughout the world were moving from coal and steam to oil-powered engines. Just before the outbreak of World War II about a quarter of the world's merchant ships were either powered by diesel engines, many of them Doxford diesels, or Charles Parsons' (page 130) marine steam turbines. Doxfords also suffered from the post war depression, despite its technological inventiveness, and was forced to amalgamate with yards in Scotland and Northern Ireland. Doxfords even closed in 1924. It reopened in 1927, but from 1930 to 1936 the yard only launched a dozen ships.

There was a massive over-capacity of shipbuilding yards on the Tyne and Wear due to world tonnage overproduction (see above) and the collapse of the world economy. In an attempt to improve the situation the National Shipbuilders Security Company was set up with government help in 1930 to buy up and close redundant shipyards for other uses. Although the famous

Reid's 1935 map of the River Wear showing the heavy pre-war concentration of shipyards, coal staithes and docks.

A relatively prosperous post World War II River Tyne. It was not to last.

Palmer yard in Jarrow had launched its thousandth vessel, the tanker *Peter Hurll*, by the following year some 80% of Jarrow's workforce was out of work and in 1934 the Company bought and closed Palmers' yard. The National Shipbuilders Security Company also closed four Sunderland yards. On Wearside in 1931 36.6% of the male workforce was unemployed, 37% of which was from shipbuilding and associated industries, and by 1939 there were only eight of the 16 post World War I Wearside yards remaining.

It was not only armaments, marine engineering and shipbuilding that suffered during the 20s and 30s – the coal industry went into decline. Before World War I coal was still the major regional export with, for example, some 20 million tons leaving the Tyne each year of which three quarters were exported overseas. Coal shipments dropped from over 21 million tons in 1922 to some 13 million by the 1930s. Falling exports and coal prices led to clashes between owners and miners. The General Strike in 1926 was instigated by desperate miners who refused to accept wage cuts and job losses.

Local companies desperately tried to diversify. Armstrongs, for example, produced cars and electrical engines but a foray into ownership of a Canadian paper manufacturing plant resulted in the loss of millions of pounds. It was not until 1934 that the government passed a Special Area Act. By 1936 capital investment by the State in the North East resulted in the construction of 'Trading Estates' with the aim of building new factories to attract new light industries to the region. There was a small improvement in the world economy and by 1939 the 'Team Valley Trading Estate' in Gateshead was employing some 3,000 people.

For those in employment, especially those in the non-traditional North East sectors of the economy, the 1930s brought an increase in real wages. As the cost of living fell, so consumer spending increased and there was a surge in the manufacturing of cheap luxury goods. Chain and department stores, like Woolworth and Boots, mushroomed throughout the region as did the demand for new plastic goods. Many high-quality, suburban houses and housing estates were built in the North East during the 1930s showing the unevenness of the effects of the depression. All these new houses had flushing toilets which meant that raw sewage and domestic waste went straight into the rivers.

By 1935 the world was rearming and by 1936 the Tyne shipyards were active again with 17 warships under construction and the Walker naval yards reopened to build the mighty *King George V* battleship. But on the Wear even in 1939 only four Wearside yards had orders and those were from a government-subsidised shipbuilding programme. But with the declaration of World War II came regional prosperity and the shipyards on both the Tyne and Wear soon had full order books.

On Wearside during World War II eight yards built over one and a half million tons of shipping, more than the 16 had produced during World War I, and the output represented more than a quarter of all the wartime British tonnage. Doxford's yard was the most prolific, launching 75 merchant ships. The mass-produced World War II American 'Liberty ships' and British 'Empire' ships, which played such a crucial role in breaking the German submarine blockade of the North Atlantic, were not dissimilar in form from the World War I British steam tramps. They were based on the *Dorington Court*, a merchant ship launched in 1939 from Joseph Thompson's Sunderland yard.

As the war progressed, riveting steel plates was gradually replaced by welding in the yards and, as in World War I, women were employed, some as rivet catchers, crane drivers, machine operators and later welders. Record productivity and outputs were achieved as the women worked side by side with the men and traditional Tyneside firms like Vickers Armstrong, Parsons and Swan Hunters produced thousands of tanks, guns and electrical generators and hundreds of warships and merchantmen.

The regional, post-war economic boom lasted longer than the one that followed World War I, continuing right through the 1950s. Unemployment in the North East was low (less than 3%) and there was a relatively strong demand for coal, still the nation's primary energy source. The Labour government invested in the region and created a North East Development Area to build Trading Estates to encourage new, light industries to the region.

In 1947 the coal industry was nationalised and capital investment by the State brought improvements and modernisation. In the 1950s, coal-mining, shipbuilding and heavy engineering were still the major industries along the banks of the Tyne and Wear, employing over a quarter of the work force. But by the early 1960s regional unemployment started to rise again.

The first to suffer was the coal industry. At the end of World War II there were 188 mines employing 148,000 miners in the Northumberland and Durham coalfield. By the late 1950s oil was becoming the nation's primary energy source: the petroleum age had arrived. By 1970 the world was consuming some two billion tons annually, half of it transported by tankers many of which were built in non-British shipyards. Coal could be mined more easily and cheaply abroad and many of the North East's long-worked pits were becoming exhausted and uneconomic. Pits were closed, 128 in two decades by the Coal Board, so that by 1994 there were no working mines in the Durham coalfield (the last, the Monkwearmouth Colliery was closed in 1993) and only two private mines in Northumberland. The North East's world famous coal industry was dead.

Shipyards and steelworks, notably at Consett and Jarrow, closed. In 1951 over 20% of Sunderland's male population worked in the nine shipyards, but their numbers were slowly reduced by closures and amalgamations. In 1961 Laings, Thompsons and Doxfords united to become the Sunderland Shipbuilders and in 1968 Austin and Pickersgills teamed up with Bartrams after producing the revolutionary, medium-sized cargo-ships the 'SD 14s' which have their engines and accommodation aft and are intermediaries between the more traditional cargo ships and the container and multipurpose cargo ships of today. SD 14s are powered by low-speed diesels and specially designed for economical fuel consumption (oil-hungry, traditional merchant ships were becoming obsolete) and 125 SD 14s were built on Wearside. British shipyards were nationalised in 1977 and Sunderland Shipbuilders and Austin Pickersgill became part of British Shipbuilders and then North East Shipbuilders Ltd, but the industry's decline could not be halted. Today shipbuilding does not exist on the Wear and the last shipbuilding yard on the Tyne, Swan

The Monkwearmouth Colliery. It closed on 24th November 1993, the last of the Durham Coalfield mines to cease production.

Hunters, went into receivership in 1993. Its status has been uncertain ever since.

Unemployment rose as the industrial power base of the Tyne and Wear declined: between 1961 and 1972 60,000 jobs were lost in mining and 16,000 from the shipyards. The government responded by creating a Minister for the development and growth of the region and 'new towns' were built, like Washington New Town in 1964, to give Wearsiders and Tynesiders housing, new factories and employment. Light industries – textiles, electrical goods, clothing, light engineering – were encouraged to the region's trading estates and the economy gradually shifted to the service sector as the old industries collapsed. By 1978 regional employment in the service sector was greater than in any other sector – banking, finance, insurance, retail, private and public services. Manufacturing was still dominated by the old industries but as Britain slipped further into recession from 1978 to 1981 the traditional manufacturing industries continued to decline as production was switched to developing and Far Eastern countries. By 1986, after a period of limited growth in the service sector, regional unemployment was nearly 20% with some areas, particularly the old industrial ones, having as much as 50%.

The story of the Wear graphically demonstrates the collapse of the traditional North East industries: the last ton of coal was shipped from Sunderland in 1986, the last Wearside shipyard closed in 1990 and the last Durham mine, the Monkwearmouth colliery, closed in 1993. By 1996 the North East was significantly deindustrialised. But not all changes have been for the worse.

CHAPTER THIRTEEN

REGENERATION: the riverside revival

Once again salmon are returning to breed in the clean and sweet smelling waters of the upper reaches of the Tyne and the Wear. It is a remarkable turnaround since, for much of this century, the rivers' lower reaches were grossly polluted, ecologically dead, impassable for salmon and little more than channels for industrial and domestic waste. For generations riverbank industries – such as glass, iron, steel and chemical works, shipyards and metal-plating shops – have all discharged effluent into the rivers. But if industrial effluent had been the only problem the rivers may not have died. The worst estuarine pollutants were organic and the main polluter: the domestic water closet!

The wealthy on Tyneside and Wearside had been served by water closets since the 1820s, but not the rest of the population. The first large council estates were built after World War I which were followed, beginning in the 1920s, by a massive house-reconditioning programme. Many good quality private suburban housing estates were built during the 1930s and after World War II the number of council estates increased rapidly. All of these early and mid twentieth century houses had flushing toilets and raw sewage and domestic waste were flushed straight into the rivers.

Dissolved oxygen is used by water-borne bacteria to break down organic pollution. Therefore the greater the organic pollution, the greater the oxygen loss and if the dissolved oxygen level falls below 30 percent saturation, salmon and sea trout are unable to survive. As early as 1920 readings made in the Tyne estuary were recording zero levels of oxygen. By 1959 the salmon returns from the river's anglers were nil and the Tyne had become one of the worst-polluted rivers in Britain. The 1958 annual report from the Northumbrian and Tyneside River Board stated: *Tyne water in the industrial belt has none of the accepted characteristics and quality of normal river water. It is lethal to fish, and to humans is probably more dangerous when swallowed than when inhaled. It was estimated that in 1959 along a 20-mile stretch of the main Tyne from Wylam to the sea each day 270*

Alfred Chaytor was one of the River Tyne's greatest salmon fishermen and author of the classic salmon fishing book, Letters to a Salmon Fisher's Sons. *His two elder sons display a magnificent catch of Tyne salmon in 1908.*

sewers poured 35 million gallons of untreated sewage into the river. In 1969 a public enquiry held in the summertime at Newcastle's Moot Hall had to be abandoned because of the smell coming from the river.

In 1958 twenty Tyneside Local Authorities started to work together to promote a cleaner river. In 1966 a Tyneside Joint Sewerage Board was set up with the aim of promoting the construction of a sewage collection and disposal scheme. In 1973 the Board began to tackle the largest estuarine clean-up ever

The clean, sweet smelling waters of the upper reaches of the Tyne.

undertaken in Britain and in 1974 the Northumbrian Water Authority took over the project: by then it involved cleaning up 20 miles (32 km) of estuary, eight and half miles (14 km) of beach and the building of 45 new sewers. On both banks of the river enormous interceptor sewers were constructed. All the separate sewage outlets that once led into the river were then piped into the interceptors which carried the sewage, mainly by gravity, to a specially built treatment works at Howdon. A tunnel was constructed under the Tyne at Jarrow to bring sewage from the south bank interceptor to the Howdon works.

In the late 1970s a scheme similar to the treatment of the Tyne's crude sewage was carried out on the lower estuary of the Wear. Sewage from estuarine and other sewers that discharged into the North Sea was taken, using interceptors, to a plant at Hendon for treatment before discharge. These ambitious clean-up schemes have been very successful and were an essential precursor to the building of new housing, hotels, offices and marinas which have since been built along the tidal reaches of both rivers, as part of the massive riverside revival of recent years.

Each year Durham Cathedral, Hadrian's Wall, the Northumberland countryside and the upper valleys of the Tyne and Wear continue to attract thousands of national and international visitors. Dramatic changes and improvements in the riverside economies have taken place as a result of the revival, even though some urban black spots remain, and the region is attracting increasing numbers of people. Today the riversides of the Tyne and Wear are bustling with life as are the high-volume, high fashion, city-centre shopping malls of Newcastle, or the out-of-town Metro Centre at Gateshead, currently the largest retail complex of its kind in Europe. Overall, the North East has achieved a prosperous appearance.

The region has a lively and energetic arts and entertainments scene, with everything from Opera to Bingo. It has large scale theatres which attract, for example, the Royal Shakespeare Company or the Kirov Ballet. There are smaller scale playhouses and theatres, which stage innovative drama pieces with performing groups from as far afield as Japan and Russia.

The music scene in the North East is particularly vital with the Northern Sinfonia, the region's resident orchestra, having a fine national and international reputation. The region has produced an astonishing collection of big name musicians of its own, from the Animals, Brian Ferry and Lindisfarne, to Sting, Mark Knopfler and Chris Rea, to more recent bands like Prefab Sprout, Dub Star and Kenickie. The Newcastle Arena opened late in 1995 giving the North East a world class venue for international stars such as Rod Stewart, Garry Glitter and M People.

The North East is passionate about sport. Recent football successes have placed Newcastle United and Sunderland Football Club amongst the most talked about teams in the land. Gateshead International Stadium hosts national and international athletics and sporting events. Each year thousands of participants race each other in the Great North Run – Europe's largest road race.

Much of the improvement in the economy and appearance of the region is attributable to both government and private investment. Since the 1930s, when the region was first classified as a 'depressed area', there has been continuous government involvement with the aim of attracting outside companies to the region. Varying degrees of state assistance have been made available to replace declining traditional industries. In the 1980s and 90s both government and private money has been massively invested in the region as jobs and new industries have been created. The new modern manufacturing and service industries were so successful that in the 1990-1992 national recession, the North East showed a far smaller rise in unemployment than in any other English region.

A major impact on the North East has been made by the Tyne and Wear Development Corporation (TWDC). The TWDC was established in 1987 with the aim of delivering projects of such scale and quality that they would create lasting prosperity for the region. It had four clear objectives: creating new business districts; increasing employment and improving access to jobs; reviving the riversides as places to live and improving and protecting the environment. These objectives were successfully met when between 1987 and 1997 some 30 miles of derelict, inner-city, riverside land, situated within the areas of four local authorities, was brought back to life. Land from ten key sites on the banks of the Tyne and Wear was cleaned, infrastructure installed and plots sold to private developers for transformation into business parks, leisure facilities and homes.

The TWDC used a 'Master Urban Land Developer' role to develop projects from vision to completion with the Corporation taking the responsibility for each stage of the developments. The essential elements of the Master Developer role included market research; consultation with the local community; land assembly; master planning the development; decontaminating what had become by 1987 some of the most stigmatised tracts of land in Britain; securing the infrastructure; selecting individual developers for specific phases of a scheme (and closely monitoring their progress throughout) and, finally, creating a training provision for local people to secure jobs.

One of the first completed Corporation's 'flagship development projects' was the £140 million, 24 hectare business park at Elswick, the site of Armstrong's factory and yards (page 150) on the River Tyne. The massive site had lain empty for over 10 years until the Corporation, in partnership with private developers, built one of the largest business parks in the North of England. Newcastle Business Park was an instant success and some 5,000 people were employed there in 1997. British Airways housed the largest 'call centre' in the world there and the Park won the Royal Institution of Chartered Surveyors award for the best urban renewal project.

A mile or two seaward along the banks of the River Tyne is the TWDC's Newcastle Quayside development. This £170 million development is an attractive mixture of office buildings, a four star hotel, private housing, new leisure facilities and public art. The Quayside development is linked by a three mile long riverside walkway which brought new life to a run-down area which was for many centuries the hub of the city's commercial life.

Between 1987 and 1997 the Corporation helped attract a billion pounds of investment, which included automotives, electronics, offshore and financial service companies, into the Tyne and Wear region. In that period many local businesses received TWDC help with the result that they were more able to compete both nationally and internationally.

The banks of the Tyne and Wear now house some of the major employers in the North East. With the Corporation's support a whole

Right: The site of Lord Armstrong's Elswick factory and yards before becoming the Newcastle Business Park. (AirFotos.)

Below: The £140 million, 24 hectare Newcastle Business Park at Elswick. (James Taylor.)

Above: Derelict Newcastle Quayside in 1980 and before development by the TWDC. (OMG.)

Below: Newcastle Quayside 1997: Keelman Square. (C. Auld.)

new generation of industries, centred around building, installing and maintaining rigs for offshore oil and gas fields, quickly evolved. Former shipbuilders and engineers became involved in the new offshore technology and Tyneside became the European centre for the construction of rigs' 'topsides' and the world leader in sub-sea pipe laying. Further improvements to the economic well-being of the region occurred when, for example, the TWDC helped bring about the purchase (by a Dutch company) of the Swan Hunter shipyard; the Corporation assisted the massive dry dock refurbishment of the Hebburn yard of Tyne Tees Dockyard and the TWDC enabled AMEC Offshore to bid for floating storage and off-loading facilities.

The Corporation's largest project is situated towards the mouth of the River Tyne at North Shields. It is the Royal Quays development and the 200 acre site is the largest urban renewal project outside London. It is estimated that the total investment in the Royal Quays site, when complete, will be around £245 million with £84 million provided by the Corporation. The development includes the site of the Albert

Edward Dock, once the main trading dock on the Tyne. Royal Quays brought 1200 homes, new industrial premises in Enterprise Zone land, new parks, an outlet shopping centre and major attractions such as the Wet 'n' Wild Waterpark to the region. Local communities benefited from the new educational, health care and shopping facilities within Royal Quays and a much improved road structure linking the area to the A19.

Two other major TWDC projects on the River Tyne were the Viking Industrial Park and the South Shields Riverside development. The Viking Industrial Park at Jarrow created 1500 new job opportunities in a modern industrial park. In an attractive landscaped riverside setting, 140 new houses were built at South Shields Riverside and an arts and entertainment centre was developed within the South Shields Customs House.

With the approach of the millennium the TWDC spearheaded a £54 million Millennium Landmark Project to be built in the centre of Newcastle, near the Central Station. The 'International Centre for Life' is one of 12 such projects across the UK supported by the

The Anasuria, *one of the world's largest floating oil platforms. The 15 storey high, 130,000 tonne vessel being fitted out in 1996 with state of the art drilling equipment at AMEC's Hadrian Yard at Wallsend on the River Tyne.*
(M. Blenkinsop.)

The site of a Newcastle millennium project, the International Centre of Life, which is situated to the west of Newcastle railway station. (AirFotos.)

Millennium Commission. In 1996 the Centre was awarded £27 million from the Millennium Commission, then the largest lottery grant awarded in the North East. The 200,000 sq ft International Centre for Life will have three distinct elements – a 'Life Centre', a 'Genetics Institute' and a 'Bioscience Centre'. The theme throughout each element is 'the gene' and the Life Centre will be an interactive visitor attraction where the genetic 'secrets of life' are explored; the Genetics Institute will house Newcastle's internationally renowned research groups into human genetics and the Bio Science Centre will provide space for new biotechnology businesses.

Significant progress was also made by the

TWDC on the banks of the River Wear. The Corporation's largest business project – the Sunderland Enterprise Park – is based at Hylton. The £117 million scheme covers 130 acres (between the Nissan car factory on the A19 and Sunderland city centre) and the million square feet of commercial and industrial property within the site (which includes a retail complex) is expected to eventually employ some 4,000 people.

Towards the mouth of the River Wear is the Corporation's St Peter's Riverside project. In 1997 it contained Britain's newest marina and marine activities centre as well as 300 new houses, award-winning student accommodation, office space and historic

The carefully restored Roseline Building, on the banks of the River Wear, is part of the TWDC's St Peter's Riverside development. (Chris Henderson.)

buildings that have been restored to their Georgian and Edwardian splendour. It is a £150 million regeneration scheme and the 90 acre St Peter's site houses the second campus of Sunderland University and a National Glass Centre which in 1996 won £7 million of support from the National Lottery. The long tradition of learning, which began in Anglo-Saxon times with Bede, will be continued in both the University and the National Glass Centre.

Stadium Park is TWDC's third major project in Sunderland. The Corporation bought the 50 acre colliery site from British Coal and work began in April 1996 to turn 20 acres of the derelict mine into a safe site for Sunderland Football Club's new 40,000 capacity stadium and car park. The remaining 30 acres will be developed as a multi-million pound leisure scheme.

Over two thousand years the rivers and the banks of the Tyne and the Wear have been transformed; dramatically in the last two centuries. The two rivers have a long and honourable history and, justifiably, the people who live and work along the river banks have high expectations for the future.

BIBLIOGRAPHY

Ayris, I and Sheldon, P — On the Waterfront. Newcastle City Libraries and Arts. Newcastle 1995

Barke, M & Buswell, R J — Newcastle's Changing Map. Newcastle City Libraries & Arts. Newcastle 1992

Bean, D — Tyneside: a biography. London, Macmillan, 1971

Blair, P H — Northumbria in the Days of Bede. London, Gollancz, 1976

Bourne, H — The History of Newcastle upon Tyne. Newcastle, 1736

Brand, J — The History and Antiquities of the Town and County of the Town of Newcastle upon Tyne. Newcastle 2 vols., 1789

Carmichael, J W — Pictures of Tyneside or Life and Scenery on the River Tyne. Newcastle c. 1830

Catchment Management Plans — Rivers Tyne and Wear. National Rivers Authority, Northumbria and Yorkshire Region. Newcastle,1994

Chapman, J C and Mytum, M C (eds.) — Settlement in North Britain, 1000 BC-1000 AD. British Archaeological Reports. Int Series 118. London,

Charleton, R J — Newcastle Town. Newcastle, 1885

Corfe, T — Sunderland, A Short History. Newcastle, F Graham, 1973

Defoe, D — A Tour Through the Island of Great Britain. Vol III. London, 1778

Dougan, D J — The History of North East Shipbuilding. London, Allen &Unwin, 1968

Fayle, E — A Short History of the World's Shipping Industry. Allen & Unwin, 1933

Finch, R — Coals from Newcastle. Lavenham, T Dalton, 1973

Galloway, R L — History of Coal Mining in Great Britain. London, Macmillan, 1882

Gray, W — Chorographia or a Survey of Newcastle upon Tyne. Newcastle, 1649

Gutherie, J — The River Tyne, Its History and Resources. Newcastle, A Reid, 1880

Hair, T — Sketches of the Coal Mines in Northumberland and Durham. London, J Madden, 1844

Hepple, L W — A History of Northumberland and Newcastle upon Tyne. Chichester, Phillimore, 1976

Hobsbawm, E J — Age of Extremes, The Short Twentieth Century. London, M Joseph, 1994

Hobsbawm, E J — Industry and Empire. London, Pelican, 1969

Hodgson, G B — The History of South Shields. Newcastle, 1924

Hoole, K — A Regional History of the Railways of Great Britain: North East England. Newton Abbott, David and Charles, 1965

House, J W — Industrial Britain: the North East. Newton Abbott, David & Charles, 1969

Hunter Blair, P — The World of Bede. London, Secker & Warburg, 1970

Hutchison, W — The History and Antiquities of the County Palatinate of Durham. 3 vols., 1785-1794

Johnson, R W — The Making of the Tyne. W Scott, 1895

Johnson, R W and Aughton, R (eds) — The River Tyne, Its Trade and Facilities. Newcastle, 1934

Kennedy, P — The Rise and Fall of Great Powers. London, Fontana, 1989

Mackenzie, E   A Descriptive and Historical Account of the Town and County of
                                      Newcastle upon Tyne, including the Borough of Gateshead.
                                      1827

Marshall, M W   Ocean Traders. London, Batsford, 1989

Marshall, M W   Fishing: the Coastal Tradition. London, Batsford, 1987

Marshall, M W   Tyne Waters. London, F Witherby, 1992

Matthew, H C G   Oxford History of Britain ed. Morgan, K O. Oxford, OUP, 1993

McCord, N   North East England: an Economic and Social History. London,
                                      Batsford, 1979

McCord, N   North East History from the Air. Chichester, Phillimore, 1991

McCord, N and Rowe, D J   Northumberland and Durham: Industry in the Nineteenth
                                      Century. Newcastle, F Graham, 1971

Mess, H A   Industrial Tyneside: a social survey. London, E Benn, 1928

Middlebrook, S   Newcastle upon Tyne. Its Growth and Achievement. Newcastle,
                                      Chronicle & Journal Ltd., 1950

Milburn, G E and Miller, S T   Sunderland. River, Town and People. Sunderland, T Reed, 1988

Nef, J U   Rise of the British Coal Industry in the 16th and 17th Centuries.
                                      London, Routledge & Kegan Paul, 1932

Osler, A and Barrow, A   Tall Ships, Two Rivers. Six Centuries of Sail on the Rivers Tyne
                                      and Wear. Newcastle, Keepdate Publishing, 1993

Palmer, W J   The Tyne and its Tributaries. London, G Bell, 1882

Pocock D and Norris R   A History of County Durham. Chichester, Phillimore, 1990

Potts, S   Sunderland: A History of the Town, Port, Trade and Commerce.
                                      B Williams, 1892

Raistrick, A and Jennings, B   A History of Lead Mining in the Pennines. London, Longmans
                                      1965

Rennison, R W   Water to Tyneside. A History of Newcastle and Gateshead Water
                                      Company. Northumberland Press, 1979

Robinson, F (ed)   Post-Industrial Tyneside, An Economic Survey of Tyneside in the
                                      1980s. Newcastle, City Libraries & Arts, 1988

Simpson, R C   North Shields and Tynemouth: A Pictorial History. Chichester,
                                      Phillimore, 1988

Smith, J W and Holden, T S   Where Ships are Born, Sunderland 1346-1946. Sunderland, T
                                      Reed, 1946

Stenton, F   Anglo-Saxon England 3rd Ed. Oxford, OUP, 1971

Summers, J   History and Antiquities of Sunderland. London, J Tate,1858

Surtees, R   History and Antiquities of the County Palatinate of Durham.
                                      London, Nichols & Bentley, 1816-1840

Sykes, J, Latimer, J & Fordyce, T   Local Records. Newcastle upon Tyne. Newcastle, 4 vols.,
                                      1833-1876

Temple, D   The Collieries of Durham. Newcastle, TUPS, 1994

TJSB   Tyneside Joint Sewerage Board. The Polluted Tyne. Newcastle,
                                      1974

Trevelyan, G M   The Middle Marches. London, Longmans, 1934

Trevelyan, G M   A Shortened History of England. London, Longmans, 1942

Tyne and Wear County Council   The River Wear. A Pictorial Survey from Biddick to the River
                                      Mouth. Newcastle, Tyne and Wear Museums, 1984

Welford, R   History of Newcastle and Gateshead during the 14th to 17th
                                      Centuries. 3 vols., 1885-1887

Williams, I   Canu Aneirin. Cardiff, 1938

INDEX